2004

How Do Your Numbers Stack Up?

The letters in your name and the numbers in your birthdate have a unique, revealing energy vibration. For centuries, people have read these vibrations through numerology.

Numerology for Beginners is a quick, ready-to-use reference that lets you determine energy vibrations based on names and birthdates. From "instant personality detection" to "total name expression," you will uncover everything about who you are and where you're going. See what lies ahead, what obstacles you will face, and the talents you can use to overcome them.

With numerology, you can pinpoint compatible occupations and people . . . know in advance what sort of energy cycles you'll experience in the days and years to come . . . and determine your best course of action to follow at any time. And after you've learned the basics, add them all up to create a personalized "numeroscope" that will give you the complete picture on anyone!

Tina - Destiny 8
Personal year 2 (2013)
Name expression 8 - (vowel vibrancy)

About the Author

Gerie Bauer is an author, television producer, fashion and beauty editor, lecturer and consultant, as well as travel professional and writer. She was producer/director of the travel adventure series *Of Lands and Seas,* and is the author of ten books, five of them on various aspects of traveling. A successful entrepreneur, she has founded three companies that research and develop products and programs. She is currently president of Great Spas of the World, a travel firm specializing in worldwide tours to spas, including New Age and Spiritualism tours of India, Bali, Thailand, and other Southeast Asia locations.

To Write to the Author

If you wish to contact the author or would like more information about this book, you may write to the author in care of Llewellyn Worldwide, and we will forward your request. Both the author and the publisher appreciate hearing from you and learning of your enjoyment of this book and how it has helped you. Llewellyn Worldwide cannot guarantee that every letter written to the author can be answered, but all will be forwarded. Please write to:

Gerie Bauer
℅ Llewellyn Worldwide Ltd.
P.O. Box 64383, Dept. K057-4
St. Paul, MN 55164-0383, U.S.A.

Please enclose a self-addressed, stamped envelope for reply, or $1.00 to cover costs. If outside U.S.A., enclose international postal reply coupon.

NUMEROLOGY
for BEGINNERS

Easy

Guide to

LOVE

MONEY

DESTINY

Gerie Bauer

2003
Llewellyn Publications
St. Paul, Minnesota, 55164-0383, U.S.A.

FIRST EDITION
Fourth Printing, 2003

Cover design by Lisa Novak
Editing and interior design by Connie Hill

Library of Congress Cataloging-in-Publication Data
Bauer, Gerie
    Numerology for beginners / Gerie Bauer. — 1st ed.
        p.   cm.
    ISBN 1–56718–057–4
    1. Numerology.   2. Symbolism of numbers.   I. Title.
BF1623.P9 B398   2000
133.3'35—dc21   99–053313
                                                                    CIP

Llewellyn Publications
A Division of Llewellyn Worldwide, Ltd.
P.O. Box 64383, Dept. K057-4
St. Paul, Minnesota 55164-0383, U.S.A.
www.llewellyn.com

Printed in the United States of America

To Bernard
My very own super power
and without whom I would be incomplete

To Cary G
Gone but never forgotten
Your lessons learned, ingrained
and strengthen me still

Other Books by the Author

Don't Be a Wife—Be a Mistress (Belmont Books)

Gourmet Cooking on a Shoestring (Towers)

The Dessert Diet (Towers)

Travel Especially for Women Series (Crown):

> *England Especially for Women*
>
> *France Especially for Women*
>
> *Mexico Especially for Women*

Table of Contents

Acknowledgements

My gratitude to:

My husband and soulmate, Bernard Bauer, for his inspiration, research, very strict editing, and total support, without whom I could only hope to be or do.

Debbie Esway, my daughter and all important 6-Vibration, so necessary to every life, and my greatest and most satisfying production.

Heather and Noah Pollock, who so influenced me with their own very personal and true-to-form numerological vibrations.

Guy Bello, my son, who challenged me constantly to "decipher and comprehend," which kept my brain cells bouncing and productive.

Tom and Lisa Mercurio, for their research of famous birthdays, and for always just being there for anything and everything.

Debbie and Frank Turciano, for the silken cocoon they provided in which to think and unwind—an oasis for the mind and spirit.

Introduction

Numerology: The Magic Key

The Magic Key implies that there might be a secret key to the door of the mysterious world of love, success, and riches. "But," you say, "if numerology could unlock that door, wouldn't everyone know it by now?" And wouldn't everyone be using it to get what they want?

Actually, numerology doesn't shower anyone with anything; it merely points the way and guides you down the right path to whatever it is you desire. How can this be? Well, let us say it acts as a road map, with all the paved roads, detours, hills, and valleys clearly marked. You simply pick your goals and follow the route the map indicates. Take it from me, a skeptic turned practitioner, numerology is a great aid to have working for you. It has been accurately charting the destiny of mankind since before the sixth century B.C., in the days of Pythagoras, astronomer, astrologer, philosopher, and first recognized numerologist—and it can easily do the same for you.

Just what is numerology? There are plenty of books on the market for those who wish to pursue it scientifically, so I need not go into a lengthy and precisely detailed explanation here. This book is a quick reference, ready-to-use manual, intended to allow you to turn to the proper page for the information you need, without having to wade through all the whys and wherefores. It's a bit like popping a frozen, ready-made dinner into the oven instead of having to prepare the very same thing from scratch. However, some explanation is certainly needed, so here it is.

Interpretation of numerical digits preceded astrology, and gamatria, the actual study of numbers, gave the first understandable answers to most universal problems and events. The Cabala, the doctrine that deals with the mystic lore of the ancient Hebrew, employed numerology as a method of determining the character and destiny of earliest man. It is said that the science of numerology was actually taught to Adam and Eve, therefore taking us back to our earliest spiritual beginnings.

Numerous incidents in the Bible testify to the fact that Jesus Christ used numerology in his teachings, even changing the original names of his disciples to match the numerological vibrations of the mission he wished them to undertake; "Simon, henceforth thy name shall be Peter and on this rock my church will be built." And so it was—St. Peter's Basilica in the Vatican.

Throughout history, and in every form of metaphysical teaching, numerology has been universally used. In fact, the ancient art of Tarot card reading is also rooted in the science.

Early concepts of numerology led to the beginnings of structural mathematics, a prime requisite for the study of the measurement and motion of the stars, which astrologers believe control our destiny and scientists know foretell climatic or seasonal changes.

In one way or another all of life is controlled by numbers. To cite the obvious example: there are twelve months to the year, twenty-four hours in a day, and seven days in a week, numbers which control the cycles of our lives on a day-to-day basis.

Seasons control our crops, and tides are governed by the moon. Even the mating of animals is confined to certain periods of time, and the gestation period in any one of them, again, is known by a definite number of days, weeks, or months; nine months for a human being, approximately two months for dogs, eleven months for a horse, and so on. Each falls into a particular category governed in some way by numbers.

If seasons, which determine the planting and harvesting of crops, mating of animals, and running of tides, which govern the action of our seas, are controlled by the movement of the planets at certain times of the year (within a numerical pattern), should we not accept the fact that these same planets have exactly the same effect on humans, who are, after all, just another form of life on Earth?

Since the beginning of time it has been known that the moon not only controls the tides but also has an effect on the brains of animals and humans alike. The light of the moon is said to release strains of madness in a mentally unbalanced person, strong romantic or melancholy emotions in any human being, and the killer instincts of animals in the primitive wilds. The effect moonlight has varies according to the emotional balance of the individual, but whatever form it takes, its definite effect cannot be denied.

We feel cheerful and lazy when the summer sun is shining bright in the skies, and we are contemplative and quiet when the planet Uranus is in dominance. Peace, harmony, and happiness always rule when Venus is supreme, and so it goes with every planet and its particular influence on the universe.

The question then arises, should we not all have the same instincts and desires under the influence of each planet, thereby dividing civilization into only twelve definitive categories of reaction? The answer is no. The reaction of each individual depends upon the personality or destiny with which we are born. Numerologically there are nine different paths of destiny into which all things fall; nine different personalities resulting in nine different forms of reaction. Someone born with a 6-Destiny will most probably react to every situation instinctively with understanding and love, whereas someone with a 7-Destiny will be contemplative and even moody.

Therefore, even though all Leos (born between July 24 and August 23) may be said to enjoy certain benefits during a particular month, as in astrology, each of the nine different paths of destiny will precipitate an entirely different reaction to the influences of that month, so that each Leo will have an even more specific pattern that varies greatly.

A month that may bring fame and fortune to a Leo with an 8-Destiny could bring only hard work and little reward for one with a 4-Destiny, so you can see that rather than a general prediction, numerology allows us a much more exact one by which to chart the attitudes or destiny of each and every one of us.

There are other coordinating factors to take into consideration as well, through which we can pinpoint an exact trend or reaction of an individual. The *Name Expression* for instance, will throw additional light on the matter of one's inherited destiny and how we will accept or reject this scheme of things.

We can safely say that with the aid of numerology and the illuminating maps it provides, we can chart whatever course we desire. If fame and fortune seem to be merely a dream, you can learn how to steer your course toward the realization of this dream. Is love and a happy marriage your goal? Then light your way clearly by circumnavigating the reefs and shoals of disharmony and misery.

Putting it in terms to which everyone can easily relate, we can say that to bake a cake a cook must know the interaction of every ingredient. Baking powder will cause it to rise, eggs make it light, and vanilla lends flavor. To mix them all together haphazardly will result in all sorts of unfavorable results. Your cake may be a flat, tasteless, doughy mass—completely unpalatable—but if you take the intelligent precaution of using a tested and accurate recipe that states the exact amount of each ingredient needed and the degree of heat and length of baking time required, you cannot help but turn out a masterpiece.

Applying the same simple procedure to our lives, we can follow the recipe (numerology) to blend the necessary ingredients (the personalities of each person involved) in the amount specified (the degree of giving and understanding that is necessary), and bake at a certain heat and length of time determined by the locality (the effect of the day, month, and year on each party) to produce a perfect relationship. It is really that simple. Why go through life forever on one path when the attainment of all your goals lies in another direction?

I must caution you to remember always that there is good and bad, positive and negative, in everything; animal, vegetable, or mineral. The happiness and success that is meant for you will only be yours by using the positive aspects of your destiny. To be negative in anything can only result in failure and unhappiness.

All numbers have a positive and negative side, but the negative can be "positivized" by knowing what to look for and what to avoid. If the weatherman says it's going to rain you automatically take an umbrella with you when you go out. And so it is with numerology. If you check your day's vibrations you know how to prepare yourself for that day. And most importantly, if you have a bad day you can manage it when you know that it's just one day's vibration and is generally followed by an "up" day.

I learned this, the most important lesson of my life, from a dear friend at a time when I could see nothing but a bleak and unhappy future ahead of me. She changed my life to one of delight and contentment by simply saying "When something goes wrong, you must think to yourself, this was not meant for me. Something much better will be shown to me if I just look for it and accept it. Look only at the negative side, and you will see and attract nothing but the negative." In the same way that a smiling face will bring out the smiles on some, a frown will affect them likewise, in a less positive manner. My friend reminded me that the moments wasted in bemoaning your fate are lost forever; whereas, if you used those same moments to go forward, happiness and success will be much swifter in coming and last so much longer.

Remember too that nothing is ever taken away without being replaced. When one loses one's sight, the hearing and other senses are enhanced. Likewise, when a romance or position goes sour, use the experience and understanding gained to apply to a better, more fruitful relationship or position, and be grateful for that experience. Do not waste time in tears, recriminations, or self-pity, for this is time you can never regain, and only serves to keep you mired down in unproductive self-pity.

If you spend $4,000 for a brand new car, you certainly aren't going to waste all your time crying over the money spent; instead you will be delighted in the car you spent it on. We get nothing for nothing. The same principle must be applied to everything we do. You "spend" months, years, effort, and emotion on various relationships. Spend them well and enjoy your "purchases."

Broken romances or marriages and financial reverses do not mean the end of everything, but the beginning of newer, better situations. If you plot your course accurately the door to these more successful situations will be opened even before the old one is closed. Step through it eagerly and embark on new and exciting endeavors. People never get old or jaded when they face each new day with anticipation and positivity.

It is important to realize that each day with its particular vibration plays a definite part in the complicated jigsaw puzzle of life and must be accepted as such. Even the quiet, less productive days have their purpose if you just realize and look for it.

A 4-Day of hard work lays the foundation for an 8-Day that brings rewards. A 9-Day of ending unfruitful relationships and projects paves the way for a 1-Day that is the beginning of all things. Each day and its vibrations means another step in the right direction and should be understood as such and welcomed.

To be negative and resentful about the seemingly unhappy and unsuccessful occurrences that are bound to pop up in everyone's life would be to disturb the balance of the natural progression of your destiny as determined at your birth. It would make it impossible for the best of things to be forthcoming. Should you have any doubt of the truth of this statement try being positive, as of this very moment about everything that happens and see if you don't automatically become a calmer, more relaxed, and happier individual. You are, in effect, then opening yourself up to the universal powers that control your destiny, and only the best of everything can result. You will still have your bad days, of course, but by accepting them as integral spokes of the wheel of life, you will not suffer the bad effects of them and can go on to the good days, secure in the knowledge that they were necessary in laying the foundation for the happy events you wish for and anticipate, rather like getting a vaccination against a disease.

Since I became interested in the fascinating science of numerology I have encountered a consistent pattern of reactions from people. First, there is the predictable skepticism manifested by sarcasm, humor, and even ridicule. But when one can be told exactly what one's habits and secret desires are, plus the prevailing attitudes and events of past months or years, as well as that of one's mates, ears begin to perk up, and skepticism is replaced by curiosity, leading to investigation that turns up verifying and unalterable facts. Eventually, curiosity gives way to enlightened understanding and, finally, fervent interest.

We can soon learn to accept the pattern of our life and adjust our schedules and attitudes to coincide with it rather than waste effort and lose patience and temper unnecessarily and unproductively by opposing that pattern. The same energy expended in negative, destructive anger can be put to positive, constructive use in other ways. Is it not just good common sense to avail yourself of the shortcuts to love and success that are yours through numerology— rather than tred the uncharted "iffy" path of chance?

Numerology gives *you* the key to your mate's or lover's temperament, ambition, desires, and inherent characteristics. With this knowledge, you know where he or she is going in life and how they will get there. You can help immeasurably by subtly providing guidance onto the positive side of the road so their destiny can progress peacefully and successfully. By knowing your mate's Day Vibration you will know how to sidestep the pitfalls, when and how to be supportive, and how to make it a good day for both of you.

Numerology can also illuminate the path of anyone you want to interact with, whether in personal or business relationships, by giving you an indication of their personality through a quick calculation based on the letters in their name. This is quite handy in determining how to conduct yourself in an interview, a meeting with a prospective client, how and when to ask for a favor or a raise, how to impress a date, or how to deal with a friend or family members on any particular day—this calculation will tell you instantly how they will respond and what will evoke the positive result you seek.

All of numerology is based on the numbers 1 through 9, since all numbers beyond 9 can be reduced to a single digit within that group. Zeros are automatically dropped. Example: the numbers 14, 23, and 32 all become 5 when added together and reduced. 1+4=5, 5+3=5, and 3+2=5. Some numerologists also use the master numbers of 11, 22, and 33 in their full vibrations, which are very powerful, rather than reducing them to the single digits of 2, 4, and 6. We won't use them here since this book is written for general use, but anyone wishing to go deeper into this fascinating science can decide upon further investigation whether or not they wish to use the higher vibrations of these numbers.

Even if you don't use numerology to actually plot your course, it can still provide a quick fix of "positive thinking." We have always heard the expressions: "Think and it can be," or "Think your way to health and wealth," etc. There is no question about the power of positive thinking. Knowing the positive power inherent in each day's numerological vibrations gives you an uplifted attitude with which to help shape your day.

Immediately following this introduction are numerical value and trait attributions charts that will help you analyze and interpret the various aspects covered in this book. Then in the following chapters you will learn how you can personally vibrate to the secret powers of numerology. So-called good luck is automatically inherent in every destiny, so I shall not wish it for you. That would be to imply what it is not: a negative assumption. I shall only wish you a fast comprehension of all that follows and the supreme contentment that it can bring you. If you do not accept numerology on a scientific basis, you most assuredly can enjoy it as a party game. In either case, read on, and enjoy.

How Numerology Works

Can the twenty-first century be just around the corner? Ready or not, it is. And, as in all things, the better prepared we are for anything, the better advantage we can take of it. We prepare for different seasons and climates, both of which depend on the numerological power of the months of the year, and so it is with the onset of each year.

Queen Elizabeth referred to 1995 as her *annus horribilus*, and how often do we say on New Year's Eve, "Thank God this year is over" and look to the new one for better luck. That is no meaningless statement because the universal power of a year is very important.

As an example, the number 6 connotes peace. 1995 was a 6 numerological year and in that year we finally brought about the first steps to peace in Bosnia with the Dayton Accord, after horrible death and destruction in that country. We also saw a peace accord signed between Israel and Palestine. New York City enjoyed a major reduction in crime for the first time in a very long time.

1996 is a 7-Year, the negative side of which is critical, unrelenting, calculating, elusive, and devious, all of which has certainly been in evidence as America's two political parties fought for supremacy and actually closed down the government to prove their own particular points. Happily the positive side of a 7 is philosophical, thoughtful, intelligent, analytical, and inventive. So there is always hope at the end of the tunnel.

1997 is an 8 which can be very profitable if observed in its positive sense which means to be wise, charitable, considerate, spiritual, and to show leadership and power. But we must avoid the negative side which indicates power madness, egotistical and dictatorial motives.

1998 is a 9-Year, signaling the end of a full cycle. It is a time meant for sorting out and discarding all the debris of the past nine years, reassessing our values and motives so that the slate is clean and ready for a new beginning.

1999 becomes a 1-Year and heralds the start of an entirely new cycle when we have a chance to start over, correct the thinking and mistakes of the past and take a positive step into the future. This is the preparatory stage for the big twenty-first century that begins the following year.

And finally—the year 2000! Even Nostradamus predicted big things for this new century and we all want to be well prepared for it. Numerology can tell us what it will mean for each of us and how to handle it.

The first chart on page xxiv shows you the specific power of each letter in the alphabet. Later on you will see how to use these numbers for quick and easy calculation of almost anything in your life, from love to luck, business or personal. (See the next section for how to use the second chart on page xxiv.)

Numerological Destiny

For a quick determination of the Universal Destiny Power for the year you were born, find the year of your birth in the lower part of the second chart on page xxiv, dropping the 19 (i.e., 1936=36) and finding the corresponding number (from one to nine) in the box across the top. This is the power inherent in the particular year that will impact on everything and everyone.

For your own Personal Destiny Power, add the day and month of your birth to the number determined for your year of birth in the chart that follows (see page xxiv, 1 through 9 in the top row). Then check chapter 1 for your Destiny's Vibrations.

NUMBERS & CORRESPONDING LETTERS

1	2	3	4	5	6	7	8	9
A	B	C	D	E	F	G	H	I
J	K	L	M	N	O	P	Q	R
S	T	U	V	W	X	Y	Z	

UNIVERSAL DESTINY POWER

1	2	3	4	5	6	7	8	9
36	37	38	39	40	41	42	43	44
45	46	47	48	49	50	51	52	53
54	55	56	57	58	59	60	61	62
63	64	65	66	67	68	69	70	71
72	73	74	75	76	77	78	79	80
81	82	83	84	85	86	87	88	89
90	91	92	93	94	95	96		

Traits Attributed to Each Number

It would be very difficult to try to remember all the specifics listed in this book for each number vibration. To make it easier for you, try to commit to memory at least the key traits. Once you learn them you will see how they automatically trigger related traits and characteristics and how they all seem to paint an almost vivid picture. Eventually, you will be able to easily ramble on and on because each trait will become permanently fixed in your mind.

After you have learned a sufficient range of traits for each number you will be able to make quite a splash at your next party or impress your date. It's a wonderful way to find out the age of someone in whom you are interested. After all, you can't determine a person's Destiny Number if you don't have his or her birthdate. You'll find most people will be so anxious to have their fortune told that they will be most eager to tell you.

Once you learn the traits well enough you will be able to see how they interact with one another and you can make more intelligent judgments. You will see how it is possible for one number to negate or enhance the vibrations of another, depending on its placement. The power of the vowel for instance, can become either negligible or very important. If it is the same as the Destiny Number or Total Personality Number, then it proves that the person is living his or her life exactly as desired in their heart. This indicates a very strong person, one who will live life openly and freely.

If, however, a person's strength remains solely in their Vowel Vibration, it means they only daydream about a freer lifestyle but don't have the strength to do anything about it. In another chapter we will go into this more thoroughly and you will see how it's done.

SPECIFIC TRAITS OF EACH NUMBER

1		2	
Positive	**Negative**	**Positive**	**Negative**
Leadership	Stubborn	Patient	Shy
Intelligence	Domineering	Tolerant	Depressed
Courage	Didactic	Cooperative	Listless
Pride	Selfish	Peaceful	Uninterested
Independent	Demanding	Quiet	Wishy-washy
Inventive	Depressed	Agreeable	Insipid
Creative	Egotistical	Reliable	Indefinite
Organized	Cold	Considerate	Stupid
Methodical	Unfeeling	Understanding	Malleable
Original	Tactless	Sympathetic	Ambitionless
Individualistic	Hypersensitive	Diplomatic	Oversensitive
Positive		Charming	
Determined		Friendly	
Authoritative		Graceful	
Aggressive		Self-sufficient	
		Efficient	
		Forgiving	

SPECIFIC TRAITS OF EACH NUMBER

3		4	
Positive	Negative	Positive	Negative
Self-expression	Vain	Proud	Stubborn
Popular	Egotistical	Sturdy	Jealous
Friendly	Gaudy	Reliable	Uninteresting
Exciting	Fickle	Conservative	Plodding
Talented	Wasteful	Firm	Depressed
Passionate	Critical	Steady	Unimaginative
Sexual	Domineering	Hard working	Stingy
Artistic	Promiscuous	Methodical	Argumentative
Effervescent	Lackadaisical	Determined	Didactic
Fashionable	Loquacious	Constant	
Sociable	Bombastic	Permanent	
Enthusiastic		Loyal	
Creative		Practical	
Versatile		Patient	
Witty		Logical	
Romantic			
Charming			
Interesting			
Cheerful			

SPECIFIC TRAITS OF EACH NUMBER

5		6	
Positive	**Negative**	**Positive**	**Negative**
Literary	Fickle	Peacemaker	Vain
Dramatic	Unreliable	Unselfish	Wasteful
Adventurous	Jealous	Charming	Selfish
Exciting	Envious	Sympathetic	Intrusive
Energetic	Depressed	Home loving	Meddling
Interesting	Temperamental	Spiritual	Picky
Flamboyant	Impulsive	Intelligent	Underhanded
Physical	Greedy	Just	Stifling
Sexual	Peripatetic	Artistic	Nagging
Passionate	Wasteful	Persuasive	Self-righteous
Intelligent	Vain	Creative	Extravagant
Enthusiastic	Inconsistent	Truthful	
Charming	Moody	Serene	
Free thinking	Sarcastic	Considerate	
Futuristic	Critical	Angelic	
Humorous	Overextended	Loyal	
Probing	Devious	Humanitarian	
Curious	Calculating	Loving	
Versatile		Thoughtful	
Free spirited		Caring	
Creative		Reliable	
Inventive		Honorable	

SPECIFIC TRAITS OF EACH NUMBER

7		8	
Positive	**Negative**	**Positive**	**Negative**
Spiritual	Lonely	Fame	Power mad
Mystical	Critical	Power	Egotistical
Quiet	Depressed	Fortune	Vain
Philosophical	Moody	Charitable	Dictatorial
Thoughtful	Shy	Wise	Depressed
Intelligent	Slow	Constant supply	Money hungry
Analytical	Cold	Leadership	
Pensive	Unrelenting	Spiritual	
Discreet	Withdrawn	Considerate	
Sympathetic	Elusive	Courageous	
Inventive	Stand-offish	Helpful	
Psychic	Devious	Humanitarian	
Intuitive	Calculating	Perceptive	
Introspective		Kind	
Artistic		Charming	
Reserved		Ambitious	
		Understanding	
		Successful	
		Sincere	
		Reliable	

SPECIFIC TRAITS OF EACH NUMBER

9

Positive	Negative	Positive	Negative
Intelligent	Loneliness	Intuitive	Over-emotional
Adventurous	Depression	Understanding	Unselective
Exciting	Wastefulness	Sensitive	Unconcerned
Interesting	Self-pity	Peaceful	
Inspirational		Sincere	
Creative		Dramatic	
Wise		Leadership	
Spiritual		Talented	
Curious		Compassionate	
Searching		Sophisticated	
Giving		Romantic	
Generous			
Emotional			
Loving			
Passionate			
Futuristic			
Psychic			
Philosophical			

International Celebrities & Their Numerological Vibrations

It's not unusual to look at famous people and wonder what made them famous; how did they know what to do when, where did they get the ideas that made them a fortune, why do certain personalities become stars when others, with perhaps more talent never make it, or certain employees get raises and promotions when others are either doing better work or have more experience and they never do?

We have often seen rather unattractive people with gorgeous mates, and the common question is "what do they see in them, when they could have anyone they want?" This is because we see only the exterior. It's obvious then that something unseen is the motivating factor—personal numerological vibrations! Whether action was taken according to these vibrations or they just happened into the proper cycle—the parties obviously reaped the benefits of their personal vibrations.

A good example of being in sync with one's numerological cycles; President Clinton won reelection on November 5th, 1996—which was his 8-Personal Day Vibration, and 8 always means fame, power, and fortune! Need I say more?

To see what makes certain celebrities tick, try your hand at some of those that follow, but remember that you have to take all vibrations into account: Destiny, Personal Day, Personality, etc.

Often a single vibration will give you one perception, but when factored into an entire numeroscope you will get a clearer picture, so go the whole route. A Personal Destiny

Vibration may give you one reading, but the Name Expression will give you something else entirely. Then too, a woman's personality will change when she takes on the vibrations of her new name upon marriage, so always consider every aspect.

The following list of well-known personalities, with their birthdays and Destiny Vibrations, gives you a chance to experiment with the various readings that go into the whole picture. As you continue on through the following chapters flip back to this one to choose a few names to do a complete numeroscope on to see what really makes them tick. It will be good practice for you and you may be in for a surprise.

Personality	Birthday	Destiny
Karl Marx	5/4/1818	9
Orson Welles	6/5/1915	9
Harry Truman	8/5/1884	7
Fred Astaire	5/10/1899	6
Salvador Dali	5/11/1904	3
Malcolm X	5/19/1925	4
Henry Kissinger	5/27/1923	2
John F. Kennedy	5/29/1917	7
Marilyn Monroe	6/1/1926	7
Ross Perot	6/27/1930	5
Ernest Hemingway	7/21/1889	9
Henry Ford	6/30/1863	9
Herbert Hoover	8/10/1874	2
Napoleon I	8/15/1769	1
Coco Chanel	8/19/1882	1

Personality	Birthday	Destiny
Lyndon B. Johnson	8/27/1908	8
Mother Teresa	8/27/1910	1
Sophia Loren	9/20/1934	1
Jimmy Carter	10/1/1924	9
Mahatma Gandhi	10/2/1869	9
Richard Nixon	1/9/1913	6
Martin Luther King	1/15/1929	1
Muhammad Ali	1/17/1942	7
Benjamin Franklin	1/17/1706	5
Paul Cezanne	1/19/1839	5
Edgar Allen Poe	1/19/1809	2
George Burns	1/20/1896	9
Virginia Woolf	1/25/1882	9
Douglas MacArthur	1/26/1880	8
Paul Newman	1/26/1925	8
Oprah Winfrey	1/29/1954	4
Franklin Delano Roosevelt	1/30/1882	5
Charles A. Lindberg	2/4/1902	9
Abraham Lincoln	2/12/1809	5
George Washington	2/22/1732	1
Michelangelo	3/6/1474	7
Albert Einstein	3/14/1879	6
Vincent Van Gogh	3/30/1853	5
Colin Powell	4/5/1937	2
Nikolai Lenin	4/10/1870	3
Thomas Jefferson	4/13/1743	5
Leonardo da Vinci	4/15/1452	4
Charlie Chaplin	4/16/1889	1
Adolf Hitler	4/21/1889	6

Personality	*Birthday*	*Destiny*
William Shakespeare	4/23/1564	2
Ulysses S. Grant	4/27/1822	8
Duke Ellington	4/28/1899	5
Machiavelli	5/3/1469	1
Golda Meir	5/3/1898	7
Wolfgang A. Mozart	1/27/1756	2
Eleanor Roosevelt	10/11/1884	6
Margaret Thatcher	10/13/1925	4
Dwight D. Eisenhower	10/14/1890	6
Arthur Miller	10/17/1915	7
Pablo Picasso	10/25/1881	8
Theodore Roosevelt	10/27/1858	5
Katharine Hepburn	11/8/1909	2
Claude Monet	11/14/1840	2
Jawaharlal Nehru	11/14/1889	6
Robert F. Kennedy	11/20/1925	3
Charles De Gaulle	11/22/1890	6
Winston Churchill	11/30/1874	7
Woody Allen	12/1/1935	4
Bette Midler	12/1/1945	5
Paul J. Getty	12/15/1892	2
Ludwig Van Beethoven	12/16/1770	7
Joseph Stalin	12/21/1879	4
Marlene Dietrich	12/27/1901	5
Woodrow Wilson	12/28/1856	6

1

Your Destiny

The day you were born certain powers were bestowed upon you that will be with you your whole life long. Since this date is unalterable, its personal vibrations shape every event or incident in your life span.

The only choice you have in regard to your destiny is to follow either the negative or the positive aspects of it. To be negative and constantly try to pursue a path that has not been predestined for you will only result in continual disappointment and failure, but if you look for and live up to only the positive aspects, you will be amazed at how easily life unfolds for you and the contentment you will find throughout your life. All the pieces will fall into place, easily and unerringly.

For example, a boy may be born with the inherent desire and power to be an attorney. His father, on the other hand, may insist on the boy's foregoing all thoughts of a legal

1

career and joining his business instead, which the boy abhors. Out of respect for his father, the boy may suppress his personal desires and do as he is ordered, in which case he can never really be happy or successful. If he respectfully insists on pursuing the law career as destined for him, his life will progress happily and successfully, as originally intended.

We have all known married couples who cannot get along because each of them is of a different mindset, intent, and motivation. They seem to be constantly at loggerheads because neither can understand or accept the other's principles.

Someone born with a 5-Destiny, for instance, would have a strong urge to travel, whereas one born with a 4-Destiny would have a more "nose-to-the-grindstone" nature. These two could be extremely incompatible if they did not understand the nature of certain compromises necessary and possible in this union.

Those of you who are unmarried can now check the destiny of each of your current dates and choose the one who is most likely to favor the lifestyle you prefer. Use this guide, too, to check the destined path of friends, acquaintances, employees, and partners for a better understanding of their aims in life and what you can expect of them in regard to your own.

Remember that your destiny covers your entire life span. Even though you may not recognize all the aspects of the path outlined herein, they will eventually be very much in evidence. Some people never recognize theirs until middle-age or after, which is true in my own case, so don't fret if what you read is not all *you* at the moment. The other all-important factor is whether one lives life according to its positive or negative vibrations. For instance: in a 5-Destiny, the travel indicated could represent progress in a positive sense but great fickleness and irresponsibility when lived negatively. Are you beginning to get the picture?

Determining Your Destiny

From the first day of your life to your last, you are governed by the destiny bestowed upon you by the date of your birth. The numerological value of this birth date will reveal to you the path of your destiny and suggest the line of personal development necessary to help you attain all you wish from life. To determine the number of your destiny, add together the number value of your month, day, and year of birth, and reduce the total to a single digit. The number value of each month is:

January	1	July	7
February	2	August	8
March	3	September	9
April	4	October	1
May	5	November	2
June	6	December	3

Tina - 7 ⊕ 16 ⊕ 1965 = 35 = 8 Destiny

For example, if you were born on August 16, 1929 you would add:

August (number value)   8
Date   16
Year   1929
TOTAL   1953

Reduce this total to a single digit: 1+9+5+3=18, and 1+8=9. Therefore, the Destiny Number for this birth date would be 9. The short method of obtaining the same number would be to add the dates this way: 8 (for August) +1+6 (for the date) +1+9+2+9 (the year) =36. Reduce this number to one digit by adding 3+6, which equals 9. This number then represents your inborn characteristic, latent talent, and moral fiber, all of which will shape your life on earth.

Number 1 Destiny

As in everything, number 1 denotes the first. Your strong sense of individuality and positive nature assure you of leadership in all your endeavors. You can never be relegated to a position of subservience. Determination is the strength of your ambition, and it manifests itself in an authoritative manner that shows your skill and experience. Your originality, creativeness, and aggressiveness breathe life into your ideas and build them into productive form. You are blessed with executive ability and can manage the organization of any business, group, or household with great ease and success.

You are at your best when you start any project from its conception and learn by your mistakes. Stand on your own feet no matter how difficult a situation may be, whether in business or of a personal nature. Always make your own decisions and stand by them in spite of advisers who are not in agreement. Developing new concepts and methods comes easily to you, and you must capitalize on this talent. Extend yourself in all fields of interest because success is yours, no matter what area you delve into.

Unless it is sensible or practical to do so, you will never walk the common paths, but search out new, more exciting ones, which will generally prove fruitful. There is no need to repeat yourself. You can take the lead in anything and, therefore, new ideas are necessary.

Select your own assistants carefully for any project. It is necessary to choose those that can do as you direct, inasmuch as your methods are bound to be revolutionary and require strict adherence to your instructions. Do not allow anyone to put you off or change your mind or interfere in your affairs, as your way is generally best.

Accept all responsibility without concern because you have the power to overcome all obstacles and turn them into assets. The negative aspects of your number encourage the tendency to become dictatorial and tactless. Diplomacy is always the best tactic with which to get your way. Being dictatorial will negate your chances of success. Hypersensitivity is another negative aspect that must be controlled. It is difficult for you to accept criticism, yet you are rather critical of others. Allow your better instincts to prevail, and you should be able to subdue these negative qualities.

Selfishness, depression, and vanity are other traits that mitigate your success. Your destiny will be one of great power and success if you accept the role of leader and play it with all good faith, understanding, and generosity.

Number 2 Destiny

As the perfect helpmate, you are the ideal mate, friend, or employee. For this reason it is best to always follow the well-trodden path and leave the trailblazing to others. You can profit by their mistakes and wisely make the necessary corrections as you go along.

Disharmony and unpleasant situations disturb you greatly, and therefore you go out of your way to keep peace and calm troubled waters. Your concern and consideration for others bring you a host of friends whom you appreciate and treasure. Two outstanding traits that count heavily toward the attainment of anything you desire are your diplomacy and tact. You can do things so gracefully that there never is much of a problem in getting your own way.

The keynote of your success is cooperation—therefore, you are most successful when completing the plans or executing the directives of others who are less capable of handling the organization and detail. It is best not to attempt to originate ideas or businesses on your own.

Always agreeable, charming, and friendly, you impress people immediately. You draw out the silent and give solace to the troubled. You will go through life with great grace as a result. Calmly and intelligently, you will master any group or environment without friction. You need never lack for the finer things in life, even though you are not aggressive.

Your great power of concentration and cooperation will draw to you without much effort the rewards that others have to search for. This rhythm is very necessary to your contentment.

You have an unusual spirit of independence that makes you the perfect helpmate, yet completely self-sufficient if you need to be. You can easily and most satisfactorily take over the business responsibilities when left in charge, or those of the household when your mate is elsewhere. You prefer to act in concert with either a partner, employer, or mate, where your duty is to carry out their directives. However, this same sense of cooperation and understanding also makes you quite efficient in whatever you undertake in a managerial capacity. Yet, in most cases your success will lie in assisting rather than in directing. Should an idea in its raw state be presented to you, you would most likely bring it to life and make it workable. This is a good quality to have since much of your life will be spent in the employ of others.

It will be your nature to forgive and understand easily, which, again, makes you the perfect mate. Should there be trouble within your marriage, chances are that you would be the one to make sacrifices or compromises in order to overcome it. The great powers you have been endowed with allow you to forgive any transgression on the part of your mate, but you must take care to avoid being so forgiving that transgressions become a habit on their part.

Negatively, in your effort to please, you can too easily be influenced against your better judgment. You can also be moody and undecided, not to mention oversensitive. There are times when your uncertainty allows others to get the best of you, and this could make you resentful.

Number 3 Destiny

Self-expression is your keynote. The sparkle and effervescence you generate wherever you go bolsters the morale of anyone feeling a bit low. This, plus the fact that you are very sociable and entertaining to be around, helps you to win friends quite easily. With the exception of the rare individual who does not understand you or perhaps feels envy, most people enjoy your company and treasure your friendship. You do realize that life is not all fun and games; and though you enjoy them as much as anyone, you see things clearly and do not waste time or energy on the unreal or ridiculous.

Intelligence and a very keen mind are your two great assets—use them well. You learn easily and quickly anything that catches your fancy; but once the knowledge is stored, you go on to other things, rather than delve into it deeply. This versatility has been the foundation of the many talents you possess, which make it problematic at times to decide just what it is you wish to express. Enthusiasm reigns for a time, and you manage to transmit this excitement to others. Then suddenly your interest changes and you quickly go on to something else.

You are used to, and enjoy, getting things your own way and doing exactly as you please. "What will be, will be" is your motto, and you don't worry too much about tomorrow. This is fine, as long as you don't become so unconcerned that you neglect doing the things you should.

With your quick wit, the words you choose may make you seem a bit too critical of other people and their opinions, and you must watch it. You could easily hurt unintentionally those you love. Wit is an asset when used strictly in a humorous sense, and you have been endowed with a finely honed sense of humor that keeps you and yours always jolly.

Words and your clever way of using them stand you in great stead in any field where oratory is necessary. You should succeed in any of these areas without much effort on your part. Language and its use is like food for your soul. You thrive on intellectual pursuits and like to pass on what you have learned to others who are less knowledgeable. Music, dance, and the arts are very important to you.

Your greatest happiness is in loving and being loved. It is an absolute necessity for you to be emotionally involved. Because of this great need for love, you are apt to be a very good mate, always adoring, always ready to forgive, as long as your mate shows you the affection you crave. You must not let this love become too overpowering or try to dominate the relationship because it could lose for you all that you seek. Sex is extremely important to you and many of your relationships will be based on that alone.

Use your many talents to bring joy wherever you go and in every relationship. Cultivate new associations continually and always be cheerful and affable, as is your wont. Your life will be a happy one if you live up to your destiny. On the negative side, don't allow sexual desires to negate your common sense or cause you to be promiscuous. Vanity and a tendency toward wasting yourself and your talents is also a danger, as is a lackadaisical "who cares" attitude, so beware.

Number 4 Destiny

The four-sided square is the symbol of this number and you will prove it in everything you do. The square block is the foundation of all things, and that is the course you will take—building everything from a firm, logical, and lasting foundation.

You will not reach out for the fleeting things of life, but tend to settle only for those that will reward you with lasting benefits. You have a great head for details and can make even the most boring, mundane jobs pay off with a measure of success. You can keep your head when all others around you lose theirs. Take this for what it is worth and channel it properly; persevere when others have tired or lost interest and you will receive your just rewards.

You must learn to evaluate every idea or product you are involved with and not get carried away with the "blue sky" aspects of them. Think clearly and stand firm where your logic dictates. Never a wanderer, you prefer to live and work in one place after you have adjusted to it. You work best when you have a sense of permanence to hang onto.

A 4-Destiny is one of justice, equality, and practicality. You will spend your lifetime working toward your goal. Even when you attain what you think you want, you will go on and lay foundations for other acquisitions. Always working, always building, so goes a 4, but you are well prepared for it with a great capacity for patience.

Method, logic, and loyalty are the tools with which you work, and this wonderful combination will bring to you and yours all the material possessions you desire. Details, duty, and conservatism may restrict you in a sense, except when applied in the most practical way. You will find your- self so bogged down with details at times that you may lose sight of the overall picture. In that case, it would be wise to allow yourself to flow with the tide and accept the thoughts and opinions of more experienced people. This may apply to raising a family as well as managing a busi- ness. Insisting that your ideas are the most practical can hinder your progress, so learn to listen and weigh every- thing before you tell yourself and others that your way is the only way.

Always ready to take on anything, you never shirk your duties. When dependability is required, you are the ideal person to do the job. As a mate, this bodes well for your marriage and in the upbringing of children, in whom you can imbue this spirit.

You can take any idea, concept, or design and in your practical way bring it to life. Express yourself whenever the opportunity presents itself, both in business or in the home. As a homemaker, you can adapt the design of any decorator or artist and bring beauty and easy living into your home. Stubbornness, narrow-mindedness, jealousy, envy, and stinginess are the black side of your character.

Number 5 Destiny

Freedom is your proudest possession, and you will allow no one to interfere with it. This sense of freedom manifests itself in constant pursuit of adventure. Your natural wit, enthusiasm, and boundless energy make this possible.

You are not always consistent in your temperament, experiencing great highs and lows; you are sometimes docile, sometimes in a black temper. However, this variance of mood always implies a chameleon-like intellect that can match the mood of the times, advancing or remaining static as the situation demands.

You thoroughly enjoy everything that goes on in this great universe. Your interest, combined with your wit and sense of humor, makes you the center of attraction of any group. Words are gems you enjoy giving to those around you, and the means by which you express all you have learned and experienced. Though usually humorous, you are by no means merely a clown. Serious subjects are also your pleasure, and you express yourself well, but take care to show your mastery of the language only in areas where your knowledge is complete. You can so easily misinform people because your way of expressing yourself orally can hold them captive, and they often believe whatever you say.

You are very sexual in thought and action, and this results in a magnetic quality that draws people to you. Should you venture onto subjects you know too little about, you may well find yourself in an extremely embarrassing position. Once made to look foolish, you will be hard pressed to vindicate yourself and you will not command the attention you are fond of.

Sarcasm and humor, though assets, can also be weapons when used against someone unable to compete—without your command of rhetoric. Control your thoughts to the point of channeling them only into the proper areas to further yourself and your career. You have a tendency toward involving yourself in too many fields at times, especially when your imagination takes over. Consolidate your thoughts and efforts and reap the benefits.

Be prepared for quick and frequent changes—moves and travel. Accept these changes with a spirit of adventure and keep moving. Yours is not a life of steadiness in any case, so leave each place or relationship with no regrets. Seek all the new experiences you can find and store the knowledge gained for future use. Learn languages and use them wherever you can to get even more out of every situation. The ingenuity and adaptability you have been endowed with will allow you to do more than one thing at a time and give double the rewards.

Your negative side encourages fickleness, jealousy, depression, and a vicious temper. You also make impulsive decisions that can be harmful. You tend more toward doing exactly what you want rather than what is good for you. Your constant need for change in relationships, jobs, homes, and other areas often leaves you out on a limb, and you find yourself having to start all over again.

People with a 5-Destiny generally become writers, actors, linguists, or "front" people involved in advertising, public relations, or anything else that deals with words or discussions. Knowing this helps you to save every tidbit of knowledge you glean from life and use it in one way or another in the above professions.

Number 6 Destiny

Adjustment is your means of getting from life exactly what you wish. You will have to meet many changes, opposite opinions, responsibilities, and unpleasant situations. If you face them straight on and adjust wherever necessary, your number promises you satisfaction and you will find happiness and contentment. You will often play the role of peacemaker, since you have the understanding and patience to see both sides of a dispute and make the involved parties come to some mutual agreement. You can see through the clouds of disharmony, find a meeting ground for both people and point out the pleasant side of their relationship. However, you must use diplomacy and persuasion, rather than force, in bringing about a solution.

The wisdom with which you mediate can also be used to great advantage within groups or organizations, as well as in family life. You can safely be classified a do-gooder in the nicest sense of the word and to everyone's advantage.

Love is the reigning factor in your life, and your destiny dictates that you teach the meaning of love to all humanity through your strong sense of justice. In your personal relationships you give strength, comfort, and lasting love or friendship, and are always there when needed and wanted. You must always have beauty, peace, and harmony in your surroundings, especially in your home. Your home and family are your immediate concern and, once you have established your brand of happiness there, you extend it elsewhere.

Unselfishness is one of your main characteristics. It allows you to teach both old and young all you feel and have learned, with the hope that it will be of some value in pointing out their direction in life. Always sympathetic and understanding, you find it easy to counsel the troubled without ever being critical.

A great connoisseur of the finer things in life, you express your appreciation of the arts by being very creative in these fields. Your home is generally a showplace of your interests, yet it expresses the warmth of your personality and charm.

Many unwelcome responsibilities will fall to you, and you will not find them easy to cope with, but you know that to face up to them and fulfill them to the best of your ability will only add to your overall understanding of life and the attainment of your own true happiness. You are cognizant of the additional strength you will acquire with the conquest of each adversity. Eventually, these adversities will be like water rolling off a duck's back and will never try you beyond your endurance. You are a great humanitarian and show it every chance you get.

Your few negatives are extravagance, overprotectiveness, and being a bit of a worrywart. You may also meddle in affairs that don't concern you in an effort to make others understand what you think is wrong, though they haven't asked for your advice. You also may not allow other people their own frailties if they are inconsistent with yours.

Number 7 Destiny

The nature of a 7-Person is to be extremely mental and introspective. You delve into everything in an effort to find out exactly what the reason is behind it. You cannot accept anything at face value, but must see for yourself that your own opinions are sound. When the germ of an idea is absorbed into your subconscious, you meditate and turn it over and over in your mind until you fully understand every aspect. Only then do you act on it or discard it. This will lead to the discovery of great philosophical truths, which you will use to your advancement as well as in the consolation and healing of the troubled. You are psychic, and often experience déjà vu, a sense of having lived a certain experience before.

Yours is the role of philosopher, teacher, and healer, but it will not be easy for you to teach unless you can loosen up a bit in your outward personality. Your reserved nature gives the impression of being unapproachable. Only those who understand these quiet, contemplative moods can get through to you. These are the fortunate ones because you have so much to give.

Your interests are mainly cultural, mental, and philosophical. The finer things in life are as necessary to you as the air you breathe. All things beautiful impress you: a well-done painting, a beautiful sculpture, or a good book. You could not live without these things to enjoy. You are the rare individual who can enjoy every stroke of the brush in a painting, not just the overall effect. Therefore, you are a connoisseur of the finest ilk, and genuinely so. You would make an excellent parent because you could teach a child the appreciation of all the beauty life has to offer, both in an intellectual and a physical sense.

A reserved manner clothes you in a cloak of dignity, and rightly so. Respect from one and all is your heritage, and you accept it graciously, as you should. Life is often very disappointing to you, and you will have to face many obstacles; but with your philosophical outlook, you will understand that life in itself is one big obstacle. Only when you undertake to overcome every problem will the burden be lessened. You will take this opportunity to delve into the hidden truths of life and use this knowledge to better yourself and your life. This spiritual and practical knowledge will be your vehicle to the happiness you seek.

Never hurry—take the time for rest and meditation. There is no need to be concerned by economics, for you will generally have whatever you need. The fate of the mystic, as for a 7, is to study, question, apply, and teach the secrets of the soul, so Providence will always take care of the material needs. This is a rare gift and should be used well.

Your negative side could make you lean toward moodiness, standoffishness, and secretiveness, which doesn't help your image at all. Then many people will find you cold and unemotional, making it difficult to enter good relationships easily. You may also be devious and coldly calculating in your worst state.

Number 8 Destiny

Your destiny will be an extremely prosperous and powerful one. You will never know the meaning of poverty or subordination, for yours is the path to all that life has to offer. Fame, power, and fortune are the three corners of your crown.

Executive ability and organizational skill are the tools with which you carve out a beautiful, serene niche for yourself and your family. They will be the implements of prosperity, success, and humanitarian deeds.

With such ability, you would do well to align yourself only with large groups or organizations; the larger the group, the larger your rewards, whether they be financial or spiritual. A great sense of authority and of what is inordinately right will help you to direct your efforts toward great acquisitions. Your interest in philanthropic organizations can be extremely useful to them because you can draw to you that which many others cannot, and therefore can accomplish so much more. The efficiency and capability that you as an 8 reflect will save many hours of time, effort, and energy that can be put to work in areas where they are most needed.

You are very perceptive and understand human nature—you therefore have sympathy for people less endowed than you. Your whole lifetime will be spent in lending a hand to anyone who needs it, and that which is given is always returned two-fold.

Courage is one of your greatest assets, and you display it often in fighting for equal rights for all mankind. The underdog is your pet project. It would be well to conserve some of the energy you expend on behalf of others and be a bit selective about your efforts.

Behind your understanding of discipline and discrimination hides a terribly destructive force that could possibly use your finest attributes—in the negative sense—for the force of evil; for power is a terrifying weapon that can be used in any way you wish. However, should the negative side of your nature persist and you wield your power in a way that is harmful, you will never enjoy the material possessions you acquire because there will be no serenity inherent in them to give you the joy that good works and honest acquisitions surround you with.

Material things will be yours without much effort, but your happiness will also be spiritual in the knowledge that you have accomplished something unique by sheer dint of your ability. Imagination is not one of your strong characteristics. Therefore, it is wise to develop efficiency and the mastering of every experience in which you find yourself in order to apply the sum total to your real goal, which you are then sure to gain.

With your great concern for others, you will enjoy your wealth because it allows you to give to the less fortunate; and this you do gladly and constantly.

Number 9 Destiny

Your extreme sensitivity makes you understand and respond easily to people, atmosphere, attitudes, music, sounds, color, and personalities. This makes you very perceptive and actuates your interest in the meaning behind everything you come across, especially the so-called dark sciences, such as the occult. All things mystic appeal to you, and you feel the need to delve into these things to see for yourself just what they may hold for you. You are also quite psychic and a perfect candidate for ESP and all related subjects.

Complete freedom to travel as you please through life is your great desire. To be shackled by possessions or wealth would only impede your progress, so you must learn when it is best to let go. This applies not only to material possessions but to relationships as well. You may easily be involved in romantic situations that are sure to make you miserable; when this happens, avoid the desire to change to somehow please your partner. It would not help, and eventually the affair would deteriorate into much unhappiness for both of you. You must be yourself and have faith that you will find the happiness you seek. Do not conform to anything but that and eventually you will find exactly what you want.

Love is so important to you that you can love more than one person at a time, or group of people, thereby experiencing the great joy of this love in so many different areas. It would be wrong for you to pursue only one great romance in your entire life. Give in to the wonderful ecstasies and sadness, take from them what you have learned and apply them to the next. Only then can you find complete contentment in a total relationship.

Doing for others is one of your finest characteristics, and you derive extreme pleasure from knowing that you were able to help in some way or offer an opinion previously unexplored. You know that "as you sow, so shall you reap"; and when you least expect it, the fruits of your kindnesses will return in abundance.

Your concern for and interest in others tends to unnerve you at times, causing you to either rise to the heights of ecstasy or sink into the depths of depression. Once you learn to control your emotions intelligently through the study of philosophy, metaphysics, and other spiritual interests, you will rise like a phoenix from the ashes and take your place in the world as a truly enlightened person. No longer will you experience depression or terrible sadness over the way people walk all over you. You will understand the reason for everything that happens to you and anxiously await the next installment, knowing that all things happen for the best. You will look eagerly for the lessons to be taught and always find them, to your great joy and happiness. Your marvelous generosity will manifest itself in the extension of these truths to all you can make understand them, in an effort to help all mankind. Feel the contentment and peace that you have been privileged to experience.

You will always be in the public eye in one way or another, and your life will be full to the brim. A 9-Destiny is the sum total of all the other numbers. Therefore, it carries all the same attributes and negatives attendant to each, making you supremely powerful in every way.

Your Personal Year

Our total life span is comprised of a succession of events, experiences, disappointments, and advances. No life consists entirely of any one of them, and that is perhaps what makes it such a challenge. We never know exactly what each year will bring. Each is an integral piece in what I like to call the "jigsaw puzzle" we know as life. Just as no puzzle can be completed if even one piece is missing, no destiny is fulfilled without the sum total of experiences in each year of the life we live.

We know too that nothing that lives can remain stable. We either progress or regress, and, in either case, it is a series of stages, one step after the other. Life is also a series of stages. One paves the way for the next, which makes every one of them important. We need the quiet times as well as the exciting times, the days of work and the days of pleasure. The intelligent person knows enough to make the most of both.

To know in advance what kind of year you can expect is to get the most out of every one of the 365 days. During a 4-Year, meant for hard work, one would be foolish to dissipate one's energies on socializing, since that year of work is necessary in order to reap the resultant rewards needed to carry on the plan.

Every year has its own particular powers that fit neatly into an overall pattern when used properly. Knowing what year to begin planning, what year you will meet influential people, when to get down to the nitty-gritty, and when you can expect to attain your goal is undeniably a great asset. It's like being in the right place at the right time, and who can argue with the success of that premise?

Since it is impossible to change the vibratory powers of each year, the only sensible thing to do is to anticipate them and change your attitude and plans to coordinate with them. It also helps to know that you can coordinate your efforts rather than pull in opposite directions and accomplish nothing. A simple analogy: if you plan a picnic and it rains, you have to change plans. If the weather report predicts that rainstorm in advance it is obviously intelligent to change those plans accordingly. The same applies to our life's plan, which makes everything easier.

To find the number of your Personal Year, add together the number of the month and day of your birth, plus the current year. Example: If the month and day of your birth is December 6, and the current year 1999, add 3 (1+2 for December) + 6 (the date) +1+9+9+9=37. Reduce 37 to a single digit; 3+7=1, which is then the number of the Personal Year for that birthday.

7 + 16 + *November* + 2013 = 20 = 2

Number 1 Personal Year

This is a very good year in which to start all new things. Not only will you find the mental stimulus and ambition to do so, but the necessary knowledge and opportunity as well. Take full advantage of it by putting every one of your talents or interests in the forefront; make them known to everyone you come in contact with, in a subtle way, and watch the doors open for you.

One is the number of leadership, so this is the year you must show what you can do. Take the reins in your club, organization, business, or home. Naturally, everyone cannot take over the business if they work for someone else, but they most certainly can demonstrate their ability in their own individual areas. Your employer is sure to notice you this year, and there could be a good promotion as a result of what you put forth now.

Homemakers, too, can assert themselves. The family, or perhaps just a mate, must be directed and cared for. You can easily show all concerned how capable you are and earn the respect and appreciation that make family living so much more enjoyable and comfortable.

Put all your plans into action now, especially business ideas. See that you carry them out yourself after careful consideration. Give a great deal of thought to any business propositions that come your way now. There will likely be a most profitable one among them.

Whatever creative forces you have within you will be making themselves known because this is the appropriate time to exploit them. Inventive or innovative ideas will whirl around in your mind, just looking for an out. Take each one out and look it over, then take it to the people who are in a position to do something about it. They will admire your inventiveness.

Travel will probably enter into this cycle for you, affording you a wealth of experiences to draw on in the future. New people will also come onto the scene, which is good, because those coming into your life this year could have a bearing on your success. Cultivate each friendship and give your utmost to it because you will find that these may well be the ones that last you a lifetime.

Keep your mind open to anything and don't frown on whatever changes occur. They will be to your advantage and signify a beginning of new avenues to success and happiness. It always pays to get out of ruts, and this is a particularly good year to do so because what you do now sets the pace for your entire nine-year cycle to follow.

Never mind the "middle man" during this year. Take the initiative and do things yourself. Only you can explain exactly what you want and how you want it done. Above all, have courage and keep a positive outlook on everything.

Number 2 Personal Year

After what should have been a year of opening new doors and starting new ventures, this is a year in which you can relax and wait for some of the results of last year's efforts to come in. At least some of them should be coming to fruition, depending upon the length of time the project requires. In any case, you will definitely see some rewards this year.

This doesn't mean that you are to do nothing at all but wait for results, because you will be getting other offers as well. Some may be very unexpected, but, nevertheless, you are due for a few surprises. Look into each offer, especially with an eye to overall benefits or those that offer a future benefit. This may be a year of promotion, after all your efforts of the past year toward that end.

Basically, a 2-Year means one of cooperation or collaboration, so be willing to hand over the reins to someone else, if need be, and give your full attention to cooperating with them, instead of directing all phases of the operation. You had your turn last year. As an employer, you certainly wouldn't want to give up authority, of course, but do listen to those in your employ who feel they have some solutions to problems or perhaps a new method that would be to your advantage.

It could be that a partnership you instigate in your 1-Year is now coming to pass, so it would be important for you to show this person how cooperative you can be. This can lead to a very successful career for both, provided you don't insist on running all matters pertaining to the business. Teamwork is the key word here.

Your charm and magnetism will be heightened and will bring a host of new friends to your circle. If unmarried, this could include your mate-to-be. You will have to use your good intuitive sense in judging the character of these people—there may be an unsavory sort among them. You can do without such friendships, especially during a 2-Cycle, because your cooperative nature at that time may lead you to participate in shady deals without your knowledge.

You will have to be tactful with older people, and this may not be easy for you. Becoming exasperated will only serve to deepen the gulf between you, so it will be up to you to be as patient and diplomatic as possible. You will gain their respect and love, as well as a sense of well-being.

If difficulties occur in your home or business that depress you greatly and seem insurmountable, take heart and go at them with patience and courage. Nothing is impossible when you set your mind to its solution. One is always forthcoming if you just look for it.

Number 3 Personal Year

Gaiety and social success are the keynotes of these twelve months, for the 3-Personal Year is meant for fun, socializing, and pleasure. Your personality will sparkle like a flame drawing moths, as people gather around you whenever possible. Good contacts can be made in the course of this socializing, so you must be on the lookout for those that can be of value to you. Since 3 is the symbol of self-expression, you can use its powers to present yourself or your ideas to those necessary to your advancement, in either business or your personal life. This is a good time to "pop the question" if you have been contemplating marriage, for your scintillating personality is sure to win over your intended. This is also a perfect time for you to see whatever you have around that you want to sell, for the market will be at its peak for you in particular.

Self-expression refers to words—either spoken or written—and as easily as they can work for you, that's how easily they can work *against* you, so weigh your words carefully. You could cause rifts where you had no intention of doing so. Words that come too easily are not always well thought out beforehand—and at a time when they are even more abundant than usual, the chance of using them as weapons must surely be avoided. Put them to use instead to win friends and impress your associates, family, or employer.

Writing is a perfect outlet for this power, even if you have never tried it before. Should you write a book, story, or proposal of an idea, your chances of selling it are very good now. If you don't have the inclination for such creativity, expressive letters to friends or relatives would be warmly received, and business letters highly thought of.

Whatever you do, enjoy it. This should be a very happy, successful year for you if you accept the vibrations as they are meant to be received. Hard, unrelenting work will be better concentrated in another year. This does not mean that you should forgo business or work of any sort altogether, of course. It merely means that you can enhance your affairs by enjoying them and making a pleasant game of everything. You only have the opportunity to do so once in your 9-Year cycle, so make the most of it.

As a homemaker or even as a general laborer, you must use this year to improve your attitude, appearance, and environment. Buy yourself some new, bright, and attractive clothes—dress in the current mode of fashion—be "with it." Change your hair style and fuss over your appearance, for the 3-Vibration brings romance and affection, and you don't want to pass up your share of it. It will be some years before the time is as ripe as it is now.

Three is also the number of sex, and you may very well find your sensuality increased immensely. This could lead to very passionate affairs or a sexual awakening. It means too that you will be attracted to purely physical relationships that you might not have considered otherwise. Eroticism will intrigue you and there is no harm in indulging yourself in your romantic relationships. But go at it slowly or your mate may not understand the sudden change in you. It can certainly enhance your relationship, so take advantage of the exciting vibrations that are yours this year.

Number 4 Personal Year

Now it is time to get busy and tend to work of every kind. Four is the symbol of keeping your nose to the grindstone. Though you may not realize financial rewards this year, you will definitely reap the rewards eventually of experience and knowledge, which in turn can be applied when necessary to gain those same financial rewards you seek in the year they are destined.

Whatever you plan to do in life, there is a period of organizing your original idea, then the actual implementation, and finally, the fruition. You have gone through all the preliminary cycles in your 1- through 3-Years and now you must really get down to work.

Establish what it is you want to accomplish, set into motion the routine that allows you to do so, and organize your thoughts and time in such a way that nothing will interfere and deter you from reaching this goal.

You may well find the burden heavy this year. You may have to work doubly hard to compensate for the lost labors of a coworker or mate, but fret not and accept the challenge cheerfully. Everything to which you apply yourself will pay dividends at another time. Expect little in the way of money, because this is simply not a good money cycle, that is, for outstanding or unexpected monies. You will naturally be paid well if you are employed by someone else and are putting in extra hours. A promotion, too, may be earned through this concentration of effort; so it isn't as though you can expect nothing at all. However, the big returns will come later.

No need to worry about where you will find the strength or determination for this effort, for the 4-Vibration is one of strength and building, You will be endowed with all the necessary powers to stick with your project.

In this year, you are in effect building the foundation for your entire future; so, with that in mind, no effort should seem too burdensome or distasteful. Though you will be building relationships as well as financial and career security, don't count on much of a romantic or social whirl. They will be a bit neglected for the time being, but only inasmuch as the excitement of the passion generally involved therein will be suppressed. It is a very good time to lay the foundation in personal relationships because they are more likely to be built on intelligent understanding and compatibility than on "blind love" or sex appeal.

Marriage takes on additional importance now as both parties recognize that it isn't all fun and games and that it requires serious consideration, understanding, and effort.

You will be putting so much more into it now than in your last cycle. Get your future aims settled between you and start working on fulfilling your goals. Though your compensation for all the work and effort you expend now will not show itself this year, it will definitely do so in your 5-Year and continue building for the next few years as well.

Number 5 Personal Year

This cycle finally breaks the pattern of hard work and building, as you begin to reap some of the benefits of all your efforts of the past year. Five is the symbol of change and progress, so prepare yourself for many exciting and surprising occurrences.

Travel is well favored, so you should be gadding about sometime during the year. Perhaps it is business, but certainly a vacation is in order after the self-sacrificing vibrations of a 4-Year. Since you can afford it in both time and money, don't deny yourself the pleasure. You will meet interesting people and have exciting experiences that will last you a lifetime.

Words come into prominence again during this cycle, and you could be very successful in any endeavor in which you must communicate with people; writing, speaking, sales, advertising, etc. If you are by trade a writer, lecturer, or performer, this cycle can be doubly profitable because it is the most important to such fields of endeavor. Five is a symbol of these trades, and anything connected with it is usually successful.

Since 5 is also the symbol of chance, you can be sure that there will be something this year that will catch you completely unaware and will be a real turning point in your life. Because you won't be expecting it, you must not get rattled as each new wrinkle in your life unfolds. Accept these changes with equanimity and explore each and every one for possible future benefits. Whatever you start early on in the year will most likely either be cancelled or postponed; but take heart because this too could be beneficial. Your finances may take a turn one way or the other and bear watching. Good stocks or investments could plunge into the red, and those that have been dormant for too long could start a very profitable climb.

With all this unexpected activity in almost all of your affairs, you can quite easily develop a case of nerves, worrying over the bad turns and apprehensive of the good ones. Stay calm and unruffled, and think clearly so you can handle things correctly.

Romance will definitely enter your life, since you will be most appealing to the opposite sex now. However, with the prevailing vibration of change, this may not end up as happily as you would like it to. Romances started now often are plagued with arguments and broken engagements, but these spats will probably be patched up in your 6-Year. If the relationship is a good one to begin with it can endure the state of fluctuation your 5-Year brings.

It is best, with this unstable influence hanging over you, not to make any permanent associations at all—business or otherwise. Don't sign anything that binds you irrevocably; it will bring unpleasantness and aggravation if the terms are broken, which they probably will be—that means partnerships, leases, business deals, and the like. Just hang on a bit, for the 5 is always compensated for eventually, and your good times are coming. In the meantime, enjoy the sociability and excitement of the 5-Cycle. You should have a good time.

Number 6 Personal Year

Affairs of the home will be uppermost in your mind this year. If you are married, so much the better, as you will be very content in that relationship. If single, you will dwell on the thought of having a home, mate, and children. Therefore, your desires may very well be fulfilled this year. Be loving, charming, and affectionate with all those you care about—friends as well as family or marital partners. You will draw closer than ever before to these people and derive great satisfaction from the return of their affection, especially from someone particularly close to you.

Six is the number of domesticity, and you will react to this vibration by improving your environment, wherever it might be. If you are working, you should take the time to brighten up your place of business. If the surroundings are not harmonious, you will be most uncomfortable, so follow your urges as they arise. Personalize these surroundings in whatever way you can, perhaps with fresh flowers, family photos, or something else you treasure. It will give you a warm feeling of belonging that is most conducive to getting things done.

A need for permanence may encourage you to buy a home or plot of ground to build on when you can afford it. It will certainly inspire you to redecorate if you cannot move. Your office too comes in for a bit of refurbishing.

As a vibration of harmony, 6 includes culture and beauty; beautiful music, art, or other forms of expression that put you at ease and make you happy now. It is a successful cycle for anyone delving into these pastimes or trades. Present your work to those who can help you, and they will be favorably impressed.

If you have always wanted to paint, sing, act, or play a musical instrument just for your own pleasure, now is the time to indulge yourself. Take lessons if you can, or dabble at it in your spare time. It will be very relaxing.

Practicality will color your affairs now, and your decisions will be intelligent ones. All humanity will be a prime target for your thoughts and good deeds. You will be a soft touch for all in need and provide a comforting shoulder to those who come to you with problems. Wise counsel will be your stock-in-trade in these cases, and it will make you very happy to be of even the slightest help to them.

Fortunately, you will not be plagued with business or financial problems because the 6-Vibration is one of protection and benevolence, and all your needs will automatically be taken care of. Make your usual effort and all will be well and comfortable, if not overindulgent.

Number 7 Personal Year

Great understanding and peace should be yours during this 7-Year, as it is one of deep contemplation and mental pursuits. It will not be sufficient for you to be told what to do; you will have to examine everything carefully and determine what it holds for you before you accept it.

Moments of solitude will be welcomed so you can be alone with yourself. These periods of thoughtfulness will help you determine the pattern you prefer to live by and how this can be accomplished. You will be extremely analytical and critical; care must be taken not to be overly so. Sometimes too much scrutiny can be harmful; certainly undue criticism can make things unpleasant for you.

Everything will move at a rather slow pace for you this year—business and personal affairs alike. Some of this will be due to your more-than-usual analytical nature. You will not make decisions quickly, and your preoccupation with contemplation will tend to make you tardy in getting to where you should be. But, in general, the year has an air of dragging by. This is where your philosophical outlook will come in handy. Keep your temper under control when things go wrong or don't come through on schedule.

Religion and spiritual studies will be high on your list of interests this year, even the study of mysticism or the occult. You will want to delve into all the mysteries of the universe; and from this can come a new knowledge that will bring you fame or fortune at another time. Self-satisfaction will be your greatest reward and well it should be. Your studies and meditation will heighten your intuitive powers and make you a more keenly astute individual.

Seven is not a vibration for social or romantic pursuits so you will show little interest in these. You will find yourself refusing all but the most important or obligatory invitations, preferring instead to be by yourself.

Distance plays a big part in your life this year. It may mean the beginning of something important to you; perhaps a new or better relationship with an associate while on a trip, a visit to a friend or relative who lives some distance from you, or something else that is not of a local nature. Keep in touch regularly and follow up any opportunities in that direction.

A 7-Year is not good for speculation of any sort, i.e., gambling, investing, etc. However, it is very good for creative work in the literary field or inventions. Your meditation will allow you to create something wonderful and profitable once you set your mind to it.

A vacation at a quiet, secluded place where you can stroll, lie on the beach, or go biking to your heart's content would be ideal at a time like this, as travel is indicated now. Be prepared too for surprise gifts of a very worthwhile nature. Inheritances and the like are very apt to be showered on you during this 7-Year.

Number 8 Personal Year

This is the year we all wait for! Eight is the number of fame, power, and fortune, and an 8-Year is when it should all come to pass. If you have had a certain goal toward which you have directed all your thoughts and energies, you can be assured that this is the year in which you will reap the benefits of all that effort, for 8 symbolizes the fulfillment of all the material goals you seek.

Business is controlled by the number 8 and should prosper in a way it has never done in any other year's cycle, but you must maintain a continual awareness of money and material benefits in order to take advantage of the opportunities that come your way now. Aside from the spiritual or ethereal rewards of this particular year, keep your mind on the financial strides you can make. For this reason, it is important to deal only with those in charge, who can make decisions in your favor. To deal with anyone less is to diminish your chances.

Your executive ability will come to the fore this year and demand that you take the lead in all your affairs. The power and freedom to do so should present itself early on in the year, so have no fear.

Remember always that the 8 is as demanding as it is bountiful in the sharing of your good fortune. Should you fail to share, you will receive no happiness from even the grandest legacy. This is your chance to be philanthropic and give of your time, money, or effort. Executive ability is always helpful in any charitable organization, and perhaps this is where you can be of assistance, if not in a financial sense.

Your personality will be all-powerful now and can sway even the most conservative of associates. Don't allow it to get out of hand or overstep the laws of ethics or propriety. You would be most unhappy if you were to attain what you seek through unethical or hurtful means.

Piddling chores and details are not for you now. Leave them to someone else and devote yourself to the more important things—important decisions, important methods of operating, important companies, and, most of all, important people. They will be in tune with you, and all your missions can be accomplished quite easily, as long as you deal at the top level.

As a woman, this can be an extremely important year for you if you are not yet married. Set your sights on that wealthy bachelor you have wished for and go after him. The powers to capture him are rampant through this cycle and should be exploited to full advantage or you may miss your best opportunity to marry well. There is nothing dishonest in this if you truly care for a man, so have no qualms about it being mercenary—it is not. If the relationship is somehow not right, it won't happen in any event, so at least open the doors to possibilities.

Number 9 Personal Year

Now is the time to put an end to all lingering relationships, affairs, or business that have not proved profitable up until now. The 9-Cycle signals "the last roundup" and requires that you put the past behind you and prepare for a whole new beginning as your 1-Year rolls around once again next year. Put your house in order, so to speak, and you can be sure that your next nine years will be profitable ones. To continue to hang onto the impossible or unprofitable is to maintain a nagging virus that never lets you feel completely well.

Whatever you have in the works, business-wise or personally, bring things to a head and either secure them or eliminate them. This is not to be construed as cruelty, for it can be done in a kind manner. But do it you must, no matter how hard it might be.

You may find you are bored with hobbies or sports that you have always enjoyed previously, or people you have spent a lot of time with suddenly seem to bore you or aggravate you over mere trivialities. When this occurs, cease any further participation, for it is the power of the 9 that is cleaning house. Some people have a way of draining one of spirit as well as of money and cannot be allowed to intrude in your life. The time to exorcize such leeches could be no better, or you will be plagued by them throughout the forthcoming nine-month cycle.

Your health comes in for scrutiny this year. Have you been neglecting a certain nagging pain or skipping physical and dental checkups? If so, get at it and start the 1-Year with a clean bill of health. You will be pleased you did, as you will need all your faculties intact for your next cycle of productivity if you are to accomplish anything.

When you have set everything else straight in your life, set about a subtle campaign of self-promotion. Use all your charm and talent to impress your superiors and the romantic interest at hand—spouses included.

With such a fine line between positivity and negativity this year, you could well fritter away your time and energies on all the wrong pursuits, and that would do you great harm. Nine is a difficult number in that respect, and it takes keen judgment and discrimination to determine where to concentrate your efforts and on which objects of affection. Ask no quarter and give no quarter. Be definite of opinion and firm in manner. Let no one deter you from your course of action. Once you have decided what must be discarded, let no one intercede. You alone must follow your destiny and therefore must clear the path of what you know to be obstacles for you.

Your Specific Month

Knowing the path that each year will take is of great value in planning the direction of your future endeavors, as we have seen, but knowing the course of each month is of more immediate value and allows you to pinpoint the efforts you intend to project throughout the entire year, toward the attainment of the goals you seek.

It is always easier to face the overall pattern of things if you can take them one step at a time. You can progress smoothly through the year by taking it in one-month segments, using the Specific Month vibrations as a guide.

For example, your year may have the total influence of a 4, meaning hard work and concentration, which would presumably preclude socializing and travel if taken in its total vibration. However, each month adds its particular influence to the year, and it is the combination of all these influences that make up the whole. These different monthly vibrations add the sugar and spice that break the monotony and give you the zest to continue.

With this knowledge you can easily and wisely expend the right effort at the right time. During a month of study and meditation, you would not be able to bring concentrated labor to the proper and successful fruition you desire, so it would be best to use that particular month as intended, and concentrate your labors in the month that is slated for them.

Romance, business, meetings, discussions, purchases, and studies can all be successful when each is embarked upon at a propitious time; so why waste effort, time, and energy by going against the tides when merely observing your charted course can bring the desired goals?

To determine the number of your Specific Month, add the number of your month and day of birth to the number of the month and year about which you are concerned. Reduce this total to a single digit. Example: If you wish to calculate the Specific Month for the birth date of December 6, 1950, add: 12 (December) +6. The total 18 would be reduced to a single digit by again adding the numbers together, in this case equaling 9. Now add this single number to the month and year you wish to know the vibration of. If, for instance, you were concerned about June 1998, you would add 6 (June) +1+9+9+8 for a total of 33, which is reduced to 6. Add the 9 from the first example to the 6 of the last, and you have 6 as the Specific Month vibration. It must be remembered that you count only to 9 when figuring your month and then start over again; January and October are 1-Months; November is 2, and December is 3.

Number 1 Specific Month

This a good month for all communications, particularly by telephone. It's more personal and your personality can more easily be projected, but also get at all those letters you have been meaning to write—even notes to close friends and relatives to say that you miss them.

If you are in business, it would be the ideal time to see both old and new customers. The old ones will appreciate your interest, and any new contacts you make will be profitable. See as many possible business contacts as you can manage. Be on the alert for new prospects, ideas, methods, and propositions, but be wary, too, of "four-flushers." You should be able to spot unsavory characters quickly enough to eliminate them and not waste your time.

Look into all opportunities no matter what changes would be necessary to make them possible. This may mean a change of pace, location, or ideas, but all prospects bear looking into in a 1-Month, which is the beginning of all new things. What transpires this month could be the beginning of all you hope to find, but don't jump into anything just for the sake of a new deal. Check out all prospects thoroughly first. When you are convinced the project is worthy, then be positive in your approach. A good sense of humor, common sense, a cheerful attitude, and dynamic action will stand you in good stead this month; they will open doors and attract people to you that will provide new opportunities and valuable relationships.

If you and your mate have been quarreling, this is the ideal time to set things straight. With the aid of the above qualities enlisted on your behalf, your mate cannot help but relent, and that's your opening to make amends. Whatever obstacle may have prevented you from getting your own way, up to now, is no longer a problem. Use your initiative and independence to assert yourself, but do so in a charming, assured, and fair manner. Don't take a stand unless you know you can back it up, and be considerate of your mate's feelings as well.

Taking the lead in a strong and determined way will bring you great rewards during a 1-Month. Whatever you embark on will be a success, whether it be a new business or a new friendship, or perhaps just a unique idea. Sit down and try to wring out of your mind even a small germ of an idea. Then explore the possibilities and jump into it with both feet. Don't put off the execution of any plans or ideas because this month is bound to bring success in whatever you do now. To delay is to undo all the good that is generating on your behalf.

Number 2 Specific Month

Cooperation is the keynote this month—not leadership. You would be wise to assist in every way other people who ask your advice or assistance. This will enable you to learn many new techniques and absorb new ideas and experiences, all of which you can put to good use at another time. Your cooperative spirit will be noticed and appreciated. You may well find yourself in the position of creating a romance for two of your acquaintances or to settle the differences of those who are spatting.

Don't let anything upset you or invoke your temper. It is most important that you stay levelheaded and logical this month, especially since some present relationship may develop into either a romance or important business relationship. A cool head and charming manner will impress the party favorably.

Since last month was your month for "doing" and taking the lead in all things, you may find this month of cooperating a bit trying. No matter how urgent a matter may seem, if you can't decide the answer easily, let it go until a more propitious month's cycle. Don't rush into anything without a thorough examination of the pros and cons. This is a month favorable only to assisting and cooperating and may not be successful for anything else.

Should friends, relatives, or business associates suggest certain changes in your usual routine, think them over carefully before acting on them. Don't refuse to consider them on the basis that you prefer to make your own decisions. They may be very useful suggestions, and changes, though small, are destined for you this month. Don't buck the tide; if problems arise ask the advice of those closest to you. They will want only your happiness and can be trusted to help. In matters of a special nature, consult specialists in that field. Don't fake your way through unknown areas or force issues.

Be on the alert for the most practical, sensible, and expedient way out of any dilemma. Both negotiating and socializing are well favored during a 2-Month. You should make an effort to see as many friends as possible, putting to rest any disagreements you may have had. Be charming and diplomatic, and you are sure to erase any unpleasantness.

Relax and enjoy any outing to which you may be invited. Take it easy and try to rest whenever possible in order to calm your nerves. The quiet and relaxed nature of a 2-Month may be a bit upsetting after the excitement of a 1-Month which was charged with new ideas and adventurous schemes. This could bring about a feeling of general malaise, discouragement, and unhappiness with yourself. These disturbances could engender a jealousy of those around you who are more active or successful at the moment. But remember, they too will have their quiet months, probably at the same time that you are enjoying the fruits and rewards of a more active month yourself. We all have to travel the path of destiny, and that includes the lows as well as the highs. When you understand numerology, you can let yourself flow easily with the tides and enjoy every moment of life.

Number 3 Specific Month

A merry round of socializing and fun is yours to enjoy this month after the more quiet atmosphere of the 2-Month from which you just emerged. You will be accepted eagerly as the center of a group with all the flattery and prestige this implies. You will be very pleased with this great popularity of yours and pursue it in every way, sometimes a bit too strenuously, which will cost you too much money and time. Ration your time for play to practical level. Too much play and too little work is unhealthy and costly.

The arts will hold a particular fascination for you. Take full advantage of this aspect. The power of words and expression has been invested in you and you will find it extremely profitable to use this wherever possible. Express your ideas, thoughts, and hopes. Someone who can help you in the things you desire will be listening. Perhaps you are enamored of a certain party whom you can easily win over at this time. Impress business associates with your knowledge and experience, for all the words will flow from you like rain. Even those who were unaware of your intelligence or wit previously will do a turnabout and lionize you now. Your optimism will be a strong asset at this time and should be expressed in everything you say. Take full advantage of this power; seek every opportunity presented to express yourself verbally and you will prosper.

Entertain as frequently as time and money will allow. Invite new acquaintances whose friendship you would enjoy—people in the business field in which you work as well as old friends and neighbors. Accept all invitations to functions that can be of some value to you in furthering your interests.

If at all artistically inclined, take this opportunity to attend theatrical openings, art showings, fashion shows, and artistic endeavors of any kind. Project your interests and your personality. Seek out those with similar interests in these fields, and you will be well rewarded with continuing invitations and friendships.

Avoid foolishness and frivolous ventures that cannot aid your career or personal interests. It is too costly, and your time and money are better spent on profitable pastimes. Reject the impulse to show off, boast, or be otherwise offensive. Since words are your strongest asset, take care not to be indiscriminate in the way you use them. You could easily hurt or anger someone. Speaking of things you know little or nothing about could be a disadvantage in many ways—the things we say are lifelong indications of who and what we are. Take care you don't say things that will paint you as you are not. Express yourself fully and honestly, knowing you are, in effect, building your character reference orally and people will judge you accordingly. Say only what you mean, not what you think people want to hear, and take pride in knowing that you will be judged by who and what you truly are.

Number 4 Specific Month

After all the gaiety and socializing of your 3-Month, you will now have to get down to work. This is a month of expending much effort and reaping all the benefits thereof, so it is well worthwhile. The gallivanting may take a back-seat for the present, but at the end of the month you will be pleased at all you have been able to accomplish. Honest work and the full pouring out of effort never hurt anyone; it is the foundation from which all good things come. What you achieve now will act as the firm basis for all you wish to achieve in the future. After this foundation is laid carefully, you can continue up the ladder of success with greater knowledge and experience.

Take this opportunity to sort out all your ideas and plans, and concentrate only on those that you can see would conceivably bear fruit in the future. Waste no time on things that can have no permanent meaning in your life. This can apply to either business or your personal life. If married, it would mean that now is the time to build solid foundations within your marriage and deepen understanding of your mate. Keep in mind that your mate will be in a different monthly vibration and you will have to consider the traits of that month when planning your strategy to coincide with these vibrations in order to be successful.

You could show your interest in the family business, help in every way you can, and try to ease the burdens of your mate, or you could plan ahead for a new home or that vacation you have always wanted to take. Put a lot of thought into what you want out of your marriage and what means are necessary to achieve this. Then get to it with all the power you will be granted this month. Success is certain if you do, but remember that it won't come within the 4-Month itself. It will be put into a "savings account" of sorts, the dividends of which will be paid later in the time frame slated for them.

Only facts are important now. Charm and personality will not see you through as they would in other months. Concern yourself with the "whys" to every situation and try to work them out intelligently and unemotionally. Pinpoint specific tasks that need work and get at them, though they may be dull and boring. Go over records and see where you may have made mistakes and then correct them. Meditate a bit at the outset of the month and determine where you can possibly make improvements in either your work or your attitude. The corrections you make may start a new ball rolling that will pay off for you another time.

Do whatever tasks you can yourself, for this is a month of tackling menial jobs on your own. Forget about hiring someone else to do them. Do it yourself. You will save money, and the effort will be good for you.

Guard against a lethargic attitude or boredom. Though you may resent having to handle the smallest details of any project, go about it with a light heart and realize that all is necessary in the scheme of things, and from each effort another nugget of knowledge is gained.

Number 5 Specific Month

Many changes and adjustments will punctuate this month for you. Be ready with quick responses and an alert mind. You will be required to make sudden decisions and adjustments that are necessary to your well-being. They won't always be of a permanent nature, so do the very best you can.

There may be changes within your home environment or in your business, but whatever they are, if you are always ready to accept and adapt, you will find that they are beneficial. Intelligence, common sense, and reliability play a big part in your advancement at this time. Choose your words wisely to fully express this brilliance. Speak your mind openly and freely, allowing your knowledge and experience to open the doors to success. Let those in authority know what you can do and what you stand for. Seek every opening to make a favorable impression. Since these changes can definitely be for the better; don't shrink from them. Adjust wherever necessary without panic. This is a great month for promotion. Therefore, it would be wise to attend to bright ideas that come to mind, or to some detail that is not required of you but will show your adaptability and willingness to work, whether asked to or not.

Choose your words or figures of speech carefully. You don't want to offend or give the wrong impression. Don't be nervous or allow yourself to be forced into a situation in which you speak out unintentionally. Relax and look forward to unexpected surprises. If you should be involved in arguments or misunderstandings, they are likely to be of a temporary nature, as this is the month of temporary fancies, especially in your love life.

Your emotions will run the gamut this month. Many engagements may be broken at this time, but don't let it upset you. A more propitious time will arise and it will be a happier occasion. This same temporary effect will no doubt color any new project in which you are involved. If you are forewarned of this aspect of a 5-Month, you can accept it without annoyance or anger, especially if someone breaks a date with you or fails to keep a promise. Getting angry will only obviate whatever good can come of this meeting at another time.

Don't even attempt to attain any sense of permanence this month, and you will not be upset when you find that affairs blow to and fro with the wind. To understand is to accept without rancor. Leave your mind open for all the experience you will gain in the many transitions that will take place. Make the most of every opportunity, knowing that though the experience may not bear immediate fruit, it most decidedly will at some future date.

Number 6 Specific Month

This is a lovely time period in which to relax and be totally at peace with yourself and those you care for. Surround yourself with a beautiful and comfortable environment. Though you will have to approach your tasks logically and realistically, you will appreciate the fruits of your labors immensely. You will enjoy particularly all that is beautiful and ethereal in every way. Therefore this is the perfect time to enjoy the arts wherever possible.

Domestic life and involvement with relatives and friends will dominate your interests this month, so it would be a good time for social or family gatherings. Take the initiative in planning such get-togethers, for others may not be in the same cycle as you and may be less interested in doing this. Parties held at your home would be ideal since you will have decorated it nicely and the effect on your guests will be a warm, pleasant one.

If you have had problems with certain relationships this is the time to iron them out because peace prevails and you should take advantage of it. After all, peace is a blessing we can't take for granted—we should make the most of it.

If you are married, you can expect some sort of change this month, even a divorce if you have been unhappy. Otherwise, it is a good month for getting married, so accept, or make, that proposal. With the warmth and charm you exude at this time you are irresistible and your romantic partner may well be inclined to tie you down permanently.

Socializing is a main factor in the 6-Month and should be enjoyed. It is also a good time to get in touch with all those people you have been meaning to see and somehow never get around to. Old friendships may hold much for you and should be cultivated.

Take care of your home responsibilities before anything else. Decorate the house, organize those domestic chores you have been neglecting, and instigate changes that will keep you better occupied and improve your environment.

Secondly, take the time to enjoy your hobbies or special interests. If you have none, develop some because they will give you much pleasure, especially the arts or all things pertaining to them. If you have no talent in this area studying it will further your understanding and appreciation.

Take advantage of the power of this month to get yourself out of a rut. Expand your interests and personality as you expand your social contacts; otherwise, you may find a reluctance to adjust when necessary to either marital or business difficulties. Carry your responsibilities in an adult manner and all will be well.

Number 7 Specific Month

A period of self-analysis will set in this month that will open your eyes to many things. You will find yourself viewing your friends, business, and environment with an analytical eye that will give you better insight then you perhaps had before. Treasure this chance to see things clearly and unemotionally and you may well be surprised. Emotions cloud issues, so this unveiling will be quite revealing.

Much of your month will be spent in more serious pursuits that will help you build toward a permanent future. Eliminate everything that hinders you—fair-weather friends, frivolous pursuits, and unnecessary possessions. Dedicate yourself to study during this period that is so favorable to such endeavors. Do not limit your scope, but follow every trend of thought to encompass all things and experiences. Everything in life—people, traditions, arts, and business—are important in the fiber of being. Only when one studies does one understand, and to understand is to enjoy life. Let your curiosity uncover the secrets and mysteries of life. Explore the mystic and the occult and you will make many interesting discoveries along these lines.

Frivolous or transitory pleasures will be overshadowed by the serious thoughts and interests you will have at this time. That is as it should be. Study and curiosity will lead you to greater truths than social pleasures or fleeting thrills.

Your intuition will be very valuable now and you can trust it to supply the answers you seek. As critical or analytical as your friends may think you are now, your judgment is sure to be correct if you take the time to see things clearly and objectively.

Patient silence will prevail as you plan and initiate all your future activities after a period of thorough self-analysis. Use the insight gained to determine just what it is you want and how to go about it. Choose the most direct and logical route and then do as you think best, without hesitation. Your way will be proved correct.

This is not a good time for speculating or for putting financial gains ahead of your better judgment. Losing your temper or being overcritical now can be detrimental to your health as well as to your career and relationships. Put your suspicions and jealousy aside and contemplate your future cooly and clearly. A vacation might well be timely and in any case you should guard your health now.

Number 8 Specific Month

At last, the all-powerful 8-Month—a month of power and success. This, you will find, will be a time when there is no need to worry about financial problems, because whatever is needed will be there. In return for this windfall, all that is asked of you is that you share your good fortune with the needy and prove your unselfishness as well as your sense of responsibility. The point will be well taken and appreciation will be yours to manifest itself at a time when you yourself are in need, whether financially, materially, or spiritually, reinforcing the biblical admonition that "whatsoever you soweth, so shall you reap."

You can take the reins personally of all affairs in which you are involved because this month is most propitious for success in everything. Should you have financial deals pending, they will most likely come to fruition now. Whatever your station in life, you must take firm control. It may mean the running of the house, school affairs, or the difficult and complicated affairs of business.

Concentrate on everything you have ever wanted in life, and the power that is destined for you now will see you through to the successful fruition of all your dreams. But this is not to say that you must sit by and wait for destiny to provide for you. Serious endeavor will be the catalyst here between dream and reality.

The time has come for you to rise up and show everyone what skill, intelligence, and determination you have been vested with. However, take care to avoid arrogance, selfishness, and boasting—these negative behaviors can make your success a short-lived one. Remember the less well-endowed than you; share your wealth, power, joy, and knowledge. Give others the helping hand that destiny gave you. Then you can truly enjoy the fruits of your labors to the greatest extent.

Last month you had to set aside all the frivolous thoughts or transitory pleasures in favor of serious thoughts and interests. That may have seemed dreary at the time, but now you will see that it has all paid off for you and paved the way for the rewards you will reap in this your 9-month. You may now bask in the glory of the greater truths and introspection you discovered last month in the course of your studies.

Your intuition will remain very valuable, and your friends and acquaintances will see that the paths you chose to embark on last month were perfectly correct and will pay dividends as of now and down the line as well. Your judgement is sure to be correct in whatever you decide to do now as long as you are thoughtful of others, take advantage of no-one and give as much as you get in whatever way presents itself, whether it be financial, physical or emotional. All deeds will be as boomerangs—whatever you throw out will be returned. So be sure you throw out only good will, deeds and thoughts.

Number 9 Specific Month

You come now to the last month of the numerological cycle. During this month put an end to habits, ideas, and associations that hinder your progress in preparation for your 1-Month, which is the beginning of all new things.

Nine governs the study of mystic or occult subjects and is a good time in which to delve into them. Many mysteries are still left uncovered and it will be well to look into whatever areas interest you for a better insight into things unknown. Your intuition during this time will be accentuated. Use it for your betterment, materially or spiritually.

There is no need to seek outside counsel, for you will be able to find your own answers and therefore your path to success. Look inside your mind and soul and cast off the bonds that keep you from experiencing whatever is most important to you. Prepare yourself to be able to step out with new and fresh determination next month when the time is right for doing so. In effect, this month will herald both the end of the old and the beginning of the new.

Because of the influences that prevail in a 9-Month— that of casting off the old—you may experience certain losses, either by thievery or carelessness. Make a particular point of checking your belongings at all times. Lock up your valuables and carry very little cash on your person; keep the rest afely locked away.

Anger and arguments must be avoided now because any fissures in your relationships could become permanent. It is of no consequence, of course, if this means ridding yourself of undesirables or those that take too much out of you.

Don't get too emotionally involved in people's problems just now. Take all conditions into consideration before making any decisions. Should people or positions seem to be drifting away from you, let them go. You are destined for many and varied relationships, all of which can teach you something, and you should be ready and willing to embark upon them free of hindrances in order to get the most out of them.

Be aware of service to others and don't shirk your responsibility to mankind if you expect others to be concerned about you. Your personal feelings may be hurt this month, but don't let it bother you or dwell on it because this could absorb too much of your time, which should be spent in more important pursuits.

Think of a 9-Month as a much-needed cleansing or purifying period. Unburden yourself and clear the path for the new cycle just around the corner. This includes relationships that are just "there," but do not add much to your life in any way. Be charitable to others, by all means, but be aware there are those who drain you and take all you can give without giving anything in return. These relationships are too negative and must be cast off to make way for those that can be more fulfilling to you and to the other party.

4

Birthdate Significance

If you have been following every chapter with us, you will know by now that every letter and number in civilization has a particular power, or vibration. There is no way these vibrations can be changed or ignored, so it is most advantageous to learn to live in accord with them.

The day on which you were born carried with it certain powers that were bestowed upon you as well. This vibration stays with you forever and is the personality that you express to the world. To know and understand these vibrations and their companion powers will help you to understand yourself and others around you. When you understand the basic personality of someone, you can deal more effectively with that person to mutual advantage.

Should that person possess a personality that is incompatible with yours, you can avoid the heartache of such relationships later on by knowing in advance that it just wouldn't work out. The following items tell you what you can generally expect of one born on any particular day. However, I caution you to take into consideration all other factors before judging anyone totally and remember that there is a negative to every positive that must be considered.

If You Were Born on the 1st

Strong leadership is your role, and you will experience the urge to lead throughout your life. You don't resent having to take the reins, and you have the strength and courage to initiate new ideas or methods and stick to them against the advice of those who are more conservative or cautious. Your mind functions like a machine that never lets up. The ideas or thoughts that come from it are very creative, for you are always building new concepts, whether it be in business or personal relationships. No matter what job or disappointment you come up against, you know automatically that you have the ability to handle it properly and jump right in, thereby reversing disappointments and turning them into exciting new assets. Learn to give a little and take care that your urge for leadership does not turn into domination.

If You Were Born on the 2nd

Your wonderful spirit of cooperation pervades everything you do, giving you the title of the greatest spouse, partner, friend, or coworker. No matter what your relationships are, you will be the one to carry out the other's wishes, without any resentment on your part, because you prefer your role. You are not subservient by any means, when you function according to the positive side of the power you were given.

Only the negative side of this vibration plays the role of the underdog. You have the unique knack of being able to execute other people's orders in a most efficient and inventive way, a trait that will carry you a long way in the business world, for it is this that is so necessary for a partner or a manager to possess.

If You Were Born on the 3rd

Rarely will you have to wonder how and where to make friends or look for social involvement, for there will be gaiety and socializing through all your life. Three is the number of self-expression and you will find yourself always dealing with large groups of people. You are the typical "Life of the Party" and people will always be strongly attracted to you. Therefore, you will have a whole host of friends without much effort on your part. Though you have a natural charm and graciousness, you do consciously strive to show these assets, realizing that your social successes have been based on them. You have a gift of curiosity along with versatility, so you can be interested in any number of fields. You like to dabble in all, but are never quite sure of just where you are involved. Instead of being a Jack-of-all-trades, you should learn to master one and try to be more focused.

If You Were Born on the 4th

You are a good, strong, hardworking soul—the builder figure in our civilization, laying the foundation upon which all relationships are built. You don't know the meaning of the word "shortcut" because you don't believe in half measures. Once you adopt certain methods of doing things, you will stick to them without deviation. You like everything in its proper place and never leave things undone. If you have been assigned a task, or if there is something to be done in the home, you get at it and stay at it until it is finished. You cannot stand clutter or inconsistency. A very practical person, you can always handle things intelligently and logically, with very few errors. You are extremely honest and trustworthy, and demand this in your personal relationships as well. You cannot tolerate injustice to anyone.

If You Were Born on the 5th

Change is the keynote of this vibration, and you will experience it throughout your whole life span. It will take the form of versatility, travel, progress, and even fickleness if you are not careful to always use the positive side of this vibration. You cannot continually uproot yourself and wander, either literally or figuratively speaking, though the urge to do so will be strong. If you determine to make a change only when it means progress, you cannot help but enjoy the fruits of life in the way you would like. Words are your passport to everything, and you enjoy anything in which they figure: drama, literature, communications, and sales. You are usually very witty, with a great sense of humor, but beware of using this wit and gift of oratory to belittle others less fortunate. Rarely can a 5-Nature settle down, and you will no doubt rush pell-mell through every phase of your life.

If You Were Born on the 6th

Six is the number of education, home, and humanitarianism. Everything you do in life will be stored in your wonderful storehouse of knowledge, to be taken out and used at another time when it is needed. You need peace and harmony around wherever you are and try to create it in every way you can. You feel it is the only way for humankind to live, and try to encourage it instinctively. Love is very important to you, and you find it easy to express it to those you care for. Love manifests itself in your attitude toward everyone you meet. Your home and family are the most important gifts you have. You continually strive to bring comfort and happiness to your family, though this often requires that you carry a great deal of heavy responsibility, none of which you really mind, for there is nothing you wouldn't do for them.

If You Were Born on the 7th

Quiet and solitude distinguish you, for you are of a very contemplative nature. Since you like to think out everything you do before making a move, you project an attitude of studiousness and pokiness, which many do not understand. It is easy to feel that you do not care about anything because you are not given to wild displays of emotion—in fact, to a certain extent they rather embarrass you, even though you may feel something deep down. The arts are of great interest to you, and you can perhaps understand the artist's intentions better than anyone. The occult and the mystic also hold tremendous fascination for you, and you delve into them sometime during your life, seeking answers that are perhaps still unknown to man. Philosophy is another of your pursuits, and this typifies your attitude more than anything else.

If You Were Born on the 8th

Material and financial matters are where you shine, and therefore you should always do well in this area. Fame and fortune fall under the vibration of the 8, and this number always produces these. Unusual strength and power are necessary to manage affairs of this nature and you have been richly endowed with both. The number 8 also brings with it the responsibility of helping others less fortunate in this area, and that effort you seem to manage most of the time. Whatever is gained and not shared under this influence will be taken away again. You have the understanding and sympathy for others that will help you to enjoy and appreciate whatever material assets you acquire. People rely on you for help and it is given in good spirit. With you at the helm, any relationship or business will be steered clear of the shoals of poverty.

If You Were Born on the 9th

The understanding and sympathy this vibration gives you puts you at the head of the cosmic parade. Nine is the number of metaphysics and philosophy, and you follow that urge by delving into the occult at some time during your life. You may even have peculiar psychic experiences that initially lead you into that fascinating study; but one way or the other, you will be drawn to it. The knowledge you store from these experiences and the study of the subject will give you greater wisdom and ever greater understanding of all the vicissitudes of life. Travel is an integral part of your life. However, where others merely enjoy a change of their home scene, you will get far more out of it than that. It will mold your character and enlarge your scope immeasurably so that you can take in all the cultures and problems of people universally and find the sympathy and tolerance that would be necessary to world peace.

If You Were Born on the 10th

What a dynamo you are! Being ten times the power of 1 you possess the intelligence, strength, creativity, and power to cope with anything that may come your way in business. The perfect executive, you fear no man or trouble. Somehow, some way, you will turn every adversity into an asset. You can get to the bottom of things and extrapolate the exact idea that will make something work profitably. Taking impossible, or at best, extremely difficult situations and manipulating them to your advantage is a great pleasure for you. Your business acumen and aptitude for leadership are highly respected, and you will have to take care not to use this power and strength to ride roughshod over your cohorts or spouse. Though it may not appear so, you are deeply concerned with your family's welfare.

If You Were Born on the 11th

A very idealistic and sensitive person, you can be hurt easily when those you care for and look after seem not to understand or appreciate your intentions. Eleven is a master number in numerology and attributes to its offspring strong powers of attraction. One born under this number should not have many enemies, for all the world is friendly to an 11-Power. You take things in your stride and do not shy away from difficult situations, but rather wade in and face up to them, thus diminishing their destructive powers. You are quick and can size up a situation in record time. Your methods or thoughts are unique and creative, and you have the power to carry out the implementation of ideas, which some numbers cannot do. You cherish the role of protector and provider for your loved ones and can even be a bit too protective.

If You Were Born on the 12th

Social life is your long suit, and you breeze through life with the charm and personality that all others envy and seek to imitate. Strangely enough, all this adoration doesn't go to your head and you generally stay at an even keel, if you follow the positive side of your powers. Love means everything to you, and you have an unlimited depth of emotion to give to every romance. Loving so deeply and needing it so desperately can lead to some heartache, but you manage to surface from the sea of despair rather quickly. You handle most unpleasant situations with intelligence and the least amount of embarrassment. This number also brings with it the promise of an attractive exterior to match the beautifully balanced mental interior. Try to be more selective in the use of your talents and charm so as not to diminish your powers needlessly.

If You Were Born on the 13th

A true "workhorse of the universe" is the title of one born under this vibration. It is not, as is so often thought, unlucky in any way. In fact, quite to the contrary, it brings with it the power of such concentration and devotion to your work that you are revered as something extra special by all who work with you. Like an architect, you must form a good foundation in everything in order to function properly, and this applies to your personal relationships as well as to manual projects. You never rush into anything without clearly thinking out and planning each and every step. You then execute them with extreme precision and cleverness, which makes for an unusually high record of success. The tendency with a number of this nature, however, is to work hard and play little, and this, of course, does not make for an even balance. Play a little, *feel* a little, allow yourself a bit more emotion, and all will be well.

If You Were Born on the 14th

Five is always the symbol of words or expression, so here we have someone completely revolving around the medium of communication. This wonderful gift is coupled with an intelligent and creative mind, so, all in all, you are a very wise, intuitive, and inventive person with high standards and morals. You know how to make your viewpoint understood and, since it is generally a valid one, you can bring others to the understanding that is necessary for full enjoyment of life. You can spin yarns of such real threads of life that it is difficult not to have faith in you—and most people do. The love of variations on any theme brightens your life with new and constantly exciting experiences. You rush out to meet each one with anxiety, but little concern for the overall pattern of your future.

If You Were Born on the 15th

Kindness, sympathy, and a willingness to help anyone in trouble characterizes you, and these traits are to be envied. However, there is a tendency to care so much about others that you often neglect yourself and get into some situations so deeply that they affect you adversely. You are quite willing to carry the problems of the world on your shoulders without complaining about their weight. Your family and home are always in the forefront of your thoughts and endeavors. For them, you would do anything, and often do. Love is a strong influence in your pattern of things, and you give as freely as you would like to receive. Knowledge and education are also of great interest to you, as well as the promulgation of equality and justice, as is the case with all humanitarians. Use these talents in any way that allows you to reach the public. Involving yourself with children will bring you great joy.

If You Were Born on the 16th

You feel deep affection for people who are close to you. You also draw strangers to you easily and find yourself the center of attraction, though you are modest in this respect. You appreciate it and steer your course in this direction, but once you have the spotlight, you display a charming, understated attitude. You possess the intellect and curiosity that spurs on the greatest of geniuses. The common, colorless, and unmeaningful holds little interest for you. You need to be inspired and enjoy a challenge. Therefore, knowledge and the understanding that goes with it are your most treasured possessions. You use them as the tools of life in a meaningful and philosophical, as well as helpful, manner. You can be too self-critical and analytical, which leads to depression.

If You Were Born on the 17th

Your inventive mind constantly churns out unique ideas that bring you all the things you desire in life. Furthermore, you have the kind of creative genius that allows you to put these ideas into working order, and that is even more important. There is no limit to what you can or will do. Anything that strikes your fancy will actuate a new burst of interest and energy. This takes unusual strength, intelligence, and vitality, all of which you possess in abundance. It also brings you a certain recognition that contributes to your desire to constantly move forward. You enjoy your solitude when you have time for it and are quite at peace with who and what you are and what you have accomplished. Strangely enough, you are also shy at times, even though you give the impression of complete self-assurance.

If You Were Born on the 18th

The most versatile of numbers is that which reduces to a 9; and 18 is twice 9, so you possess twice the powers of one with a single 9 influence. That means you can do everything that anyone else can do and more. Your interests run in every direction, and your talent is unlimited. There is truly nothing you cannot do if you set your mind to it. Understanding all things and all people adds to your great charisma and the intelligence you possess. You use your talent wisely, not only for your own benefit but for others as well. Since you do everything so easily and so well, you do not always have patience with those who do not. You feel because you can comprehend an idea or theory, everyone else should. A little more patience is required here. You have the powers to make people understand—use them, for you could well be a "Pied Piper."

If You Were Born on the 19th

An adventuresome spirit causes you at times to pick up and wander from home base, either physically or mentally. You have the faculty for carrying out the ideas or methods of others perhaps better than anyone else. You know every facet of your work and can step into any area and function perfectly because you pay attention to all phases of the operation. At home this means that you can take over should your mate be away and unable to help you. This ability broadens your interest, understanding, and knowledge so that you have a finely honed sense of judgment. You feel things deeply and do not hesitate to express that feeling in either words or action. One moment you may experience deep love and the next shattering hate, running the full gamut of emotion. Ever moving, ever experiencing, new life is infused into every day.

If You Were Born on the 20th

Completely self-sacrificing, you must beware of giving so much of yourself that you have no strength left for your own use. You are known to be the most sympathetic and understanding of humans; so people pour their troubles out to you automatically, seeking help and comfort, which they always get. There is never any resentment on your part because you enjoy giving as you do, which is why you do not know when to draw in the reins a bit. Your own comfort is the last to be satisfied. You are warm, loving, gentle, understanding, and magnanimous, all traits which are said to be divine; and surely your powers are divine for your devotion and loyalty are seldom found in the world today. The soul of cooperation, you are an ideal parent, mate, friend, or partner, and if you were a politician we could all rest easy.

If You Were Born on the 21st

Though you are the proverbial "social butterfly" you are not as shallow and witless as the title might imply. You do enjoy an active, cheerful social life, but your enjoyment extends to the people themselves, not just the gaiety that abounds. You are deeply interested in people—large groups of them at a time. You fit in anywhere and never have trouble getting along as it comes quite naturally to you. In fact, you are quite often the center of attention, which you carry off well. Heavy or deep discussions are not your interest, though you have the intelligence to perceive the point being made. You prefer to keep things light and gay. Many talents are yours and you use them to advantage, especially your talent for oratory. Words, as with all 3-influenced people, are to you what the harpsichord was to Bach. You use them like a paintbrush, painting life as you see it, which is generally gay, bright, and airy.

If You Were Born on the 22nd

The supreme builder, you are the architect of the universe. Nothing around you can be mismatched, unplanned, or helter-skelter. You must plan everything you do and then meticulously carry out those plans personally, adhering to every detail. You also have been endowed with the kind of strength, power, and tenacity that is. necessary for such building. You have complete faith in what you do and let no one cause you to doubt your efforts or the efficacy of your method. You can achieve anything you like by dint of sheer stick-to-it-iveness. However, this is also the number of *partial harvest* and therefore your material wealth will not be overwhelming. Let this not deter you, for the knowledge and skill you have can be of great value to someone with whom you are involved who has the power of making material gains. The combination of the two can be most profitable.

If You Were Born on the 23rd

Two influences here shape your life—change and words. The change can be interpreted in several ways—travel, unpredictability, versatility, or irresponsibility—depending upon whether you utilize the negative or positive aspects of the power inherited. The influence is an important one because it brings with it the power of total expression and persuasion. You would be excellent at speaking, acting, or performing in any way, literary pursuits, radio, selling, or teaching. You could easily sway the masses with your marvelous powers and should be careful that they are used only for good. All of these things add up to a totally fascinating and exciting individual, and you should be much in demand by your friends. You are affectionate and do not hesitate to express your feelings—but you cannot be tied down or confined in any way, or you rebel. Speed, too, is important to you.

If You Were Born on the 24th

The 2-Vibration of this number brings with it all the spirit of cooperation and dedicated assistance, while the 4 indicates the vibrations of solidarity, hard work, determination, and trust, so you have a good combination as a meaningful human being. You put all of your efforts into good works and work hard at everything you do—sometimes a bit too hard, I'm afraid. You do not allow yourself too much play and really should let up occasionally and let your hair down. Your home and family take first place in your thoughts, efforts, and affections. Everything is for them and you could never let anything intrude on your relationship. You can be quite content relaxing with them at home and need nothing else. You enjoy the beauty of the things around you and strive to create as much as you can in everything, wherever that might be—in the home or your place of work.

If You Were Born on the 25th

Patience and contemplation characterize you, and your life will be one of careful thought and consideration before acting on anything at all. This may give the impression that you are as slow as a snail, but it is only the effect of your desire to consider every facet of a situation before committing yourself. Many times you will be deep in thought on some subject with which you are enthralled and forget to get to an appointment on time. You have an unusual understanding of mystical things and are drawn to studies of such things. The highest of ideals are yours, and trust, honesty, and loyalty are the foundation upon which you build relationships. Though others may not easily understand you, you have no doubts about yourself and see things clearly and intellectually. There are no highs and lows constantly reflecting in your emotions, for you can keep an even keel in that department.

If You Were Born on the 26th

You are a strong, ambitious, and intelligent person, and you put these attributes to very good use in either the business world or your home life. You have the executive ability to handle big business or charitable groups to which you might belong. The 6 in your birth date endows you with the desire to teach and the love of home and family. The 2 brings the concentration and technical skill you need to carry out big business operations. The combination of the two steers you toward the fame and fortune that should be yours. Since the power of the fame and fortune influence requires that you share, the 2 in your date gives you the means by which to do so, and the 6 the desire—a most satisfying combination and a rewarding one at that.

If You Were Born on the 27th

Versatility and variety characterize you, for your interests are universal. You are continually searching out the unusual and interesting subject or field of endeavor in which to get involved. Therefore, your experiences in life are many and fascinating, which you can pass on to others to help to broaden their scope of understanding. The occult and mystic also appeal to you at some time during your life, and your understanding of these mysteries allows you to enlighten those who are less inclined. You enjoy anything that has to do with travel or the future and do not hesitate to initiate plans or projects that will not come to pass for some time to come, where others may shy away from such long term projects. Your mind is quick, imaginative, and creative, and you can quickly translate ideas of a fantasy nature into reality. Contemplation is also your favorite form of relaxation; in fact, you tend toward it a bit too much.

If You Were Born on the 28th

There is no doubt that you will always be the leader in any group or relationship of which you are a member. You know well how to take over in any situation and straighten things out or direct them toward a successful culmination. Your originality and creativity put you out ahead of the pack, and your organizational ability lets you put your ideas into practical motion. With a partner you are dynamic, for you thrive on the cooperative spirit and you like to have someone on whom to bounce off your ideas and methods. In fact, you function best this way. You need warm relationships and should not get so involved with other things that you out-step them. When this happens, hold up a bit and see where you are losing them, then backtrack. Friendships are too important to you to risk losing them.

If You Were Born on the 29th

A social gadabout, you find your contentment in being with large groups of people whenever possible. You lend assistance when it suits you on an intellectual basis rather than an emotional one; however, you do have an innate understanding of the problems of others. Your mind encompasses the universe, and there is no subject beyond your ken. If you don't know anything about a subject that is interesting to you or necessary to your work or relationships, you delve into it until you know all you need to know. Never at a loss for friends, people automatically are drawn to you, for they find your vast experience and various interests fascinating. This interest in you suits you to a tee, and the negative-minded 29 may become egotistical as a result. Your home and its protection are a major interest.

If You Were Born on the 30th

Self-expression is paramount to you, and you must always say what you feel or think. Love is extremely important, and again this must be expressed in the most romantic of

terms. Social life, too, is extremely important, and you
must always be surrounded by people. The positive aspects
of this vibration lead you to an intelligent application of
the magnetism of your personality into more fruitful chan-
nels. You should do well in any career that utilizes your
marvelous sense of humor and rhetoric. As the head of
some large group, you can command attention and therefore achieve the aims set down by that organization, where
a less expressive person may fall short of those aims. Talent
and charm are yours in abundance; use them to achieve
lasting goals.

If You Were Born on the 31st

Follow your intuition and you will generally follow the
right path to success, for you have a discriminatory sense
that allows you to judge every situation. Since you are also
honest and trustworthy, you are an asset to any partner,
spouse, or organization. Creative ideas are easily carried
out to the finest and most practical detail because your
mind is well balanced and in good order. You do not know
the meaning of the word "clutter." Everything must be in its
place, and there are definite methods for accomplishing
any end as far as you are concerned. You believe that frittering away mental energies is a disgrace, and you have no
patience with such actions. Your finer talents make you a
good choice for the head of any home or group. Your concern for others is always placed before your own. It might
be better to give yourself a thought occasionally.

5

Your Individual Day

There are times in everyone's life when a certain day means something extremely important. It may be a business appointment, applying for a position, asking for a pay increase, or proposing marriage. Naturally you want everything to go just right and therefore you can't help but worry. What should you say? What is the best way to state your case? What attitude should you assume? Trying questions, indeed, when something can either make or break your future.

By determining what vibrations that particular day will have and what powers will be yours, you can quite easily plot your strategy and relax, knowing that you have everything well in hand. Of course, if you also check to see what the Individual Day of the other person is as well, you will know what their mood is, to what they will react favorably, and what not to say or do. If good vibrations are just not with you, it would be best to postpone the meeting and schedule it for a more likely day, so that nothing can be used against you.

To determine the number value of your Individual Day, compute the following (keeping in mind that the numbers in numerology only go up to 9 and then repeat, so January becomes 1, and so on up to September. Then October begins again at 1, etc.):

The number value of your birth month   =

The number value of the day of your birth =

The current year   =

The number value of the current month   =

The number value of the current day   =

If you want to project this computing to a day some time in the future, you merely insert the number value of the month and day of the occasion in question. Let us say you wish to find the vibration for September 8, 1997. You would compute thusly: The number value of the year, month, and day would be: $9+8+1+9+9+7=43=7$, which is then added to the number value of your birth month and day to get the vibrations for your Individual Day. Remember that when computing the vibration of an Individual Day that vibration holds only for that day. You must recompute the vibration whenever the dates change.

Number 1 Individual Day

The number one always signifies the beginning of anything, which means that this is an excellent day for you to get busy and accomplish something. You will find the energy and ambition as you awake, ready to start on the daily routine, feeling full of vim and vigor and the desire to "lick the world."

You can now forget all the turmoil or unsuccessful projects of the past nine-day cycle and begin anew, with strong determination to make this new cycle a most fruitful one indeed. It is always a pleasant feeling to know you can start over and take another crack at the things you didn't quite manage to succeed at before, so get to it.

One is always a business vibration, so put all your time and effort into it and try to accomplish one major development on this day, no matter what your status in life. As an employer, you should have creative ideas that you can implement immediately. If you work for someone else you can still use the same creativity and bring it to the attention of the person in a position to carry it through. This can also be the day for seeking an advance or raise in salary, since you stand a very good chance of getting it.

If sales is your line, get out today and meet new customers. You are bound to make big sales and open new accounts. Interviews with people of importance are on the list of things to do if your business falls into such a category.

Creativity will flow through in many ways—don't ignore it. This could take the form of ideas or crafts of some sort. It will suit you to indulge in whatever your fancy dictates, and even that could open new doors.

Whatever you do, there must be some way for you to expand, and this is the perfect day for you to do so. Even a homebody can use this power to expand her or his interests by signing up for a course of some kind, making new friends, joining an organization, planting or rearranging a garden, going on a trip, or reading a new book.

Expansion of your activities will bring an expansion of your prestige in both business and social circles. Meet people with charm and sincerity. Forget old arguments or grudges—they have yet to bring happiness to anyone. "Forgive and forget" should be your motto, and this is the best time to do so. When you do, there will be an ever-widening circle of admirers and a sense of inner peace gained that you can never have when you are beset with ill feelings toward anyone. Be patient, tolerant, calm, and determined and let no one or nothing upset you or it will undo whatever good you may have accomplished.

Number 2 Individual Day

You know by now that 2 is always the number of cooperation, so you won't want to throw your weight around today. Leave decisions to others: your employer, partner, friend, or mate. This doesn't mean that you must be lackadaisical and unconcerned, however, because it is important for you to assist and coordinate their plans in every way you can. They will be impressed with your give-and-take attitude and show their appreciation in loyalty. Be tactful if you disagree and try to steer them around to the correct thought or method without imposing your will or being dictatorial. Tact and diplomacy are called for.

No matter how dynamic and effervescent you are normally, be subdued and let others take the spotlight for a change. Listen instead of being the featured performer, encourage anyone with whom you come in contact with wherever it is called for. Listening is always a good way to learn in any case, even if it's not world-shattering information. When you are in repose and pay attention to people, you will find you learn something about *them*. Perhaps you will see something you never gave them a chance to demonstrate before.

Things will take their time for you today. No rushing or hustle and bustle are indicated, and you should not allow yourself to be drawn into such a situation. When rushed on a 2-Day, one often makes the wrong decision or move.

Two is also a number indicative of working well with women. If you follow the spirit of cooperation that prevails for you today, you will find that anything involving the female members of your business or family will run smoothly. It's a good time to ask for that favor you have been wanting. Shopping had better wait for another day; you can always make do with what you have for the time being. Spend the time instead on other things, such as something you may have started yesterday, a 1-Day.

Be charming, discriminating, tactful, and helpful. If there is a marriage proposal in the offing, this would be a good day to accept it—after all, marriage is one long stint of cooperation, is it not?

Your inner instincts will dictate what's right for you today. It would be a good idea to follow them because intuition will be strong now. However, if you react in a negative sense and are argumentative or act in any way contrary to the vibrations of the cooperative 2-power, it will work against you. Take it easy, relax, and be happy.

Number 3 Individual Day

"Personality plus" will be your strength today, and you should shine like the brightest star. Express everything that is in you since 3 is the personification of self-expression. Be happy, gay, loving, charming, and exciting. People will be drawn to you like metal to a magnet. With such an attraction going for you, what better day for socializing or asking for that position you have wanted, or even seeking a raise in salary?

Go to parties, luncheons, or dinners. Be active with organizations or companies; all aspects are well favored. Should your 3-Day fall on a weekend or other day of leisure, don't sit around the house and relax; you can do that another day. Go to the club, get out on the golf course, tennis courts, or any other place where there are sure to be groups of people. As a homebody, this would be a fine day for inviting friends over or going on a shopping spree. Your taste is apt to be exceptionally good today, since self-expression is highlighted. Why not buy those birthday, wedding, or holiday gifts that you will be needing soon? With your special vibrations for appropriate selection today, better now than on a day when you won't really feel up to it—you are more apt to make the impression you wish.

Romance and affection also come to the fore, and you will undoubtedly feel extremely loving toward those you care for. Express all that you feel, and they will return your love two-fold. Everyone enjoys warmth and affection, and those you bestow it upon today will be very grateful, as it will rekindle or strengthen the bonds between you.

Worries or serious subjects should be set aside, for this is a day of contentment and joy. Whatever happens, accept it with this spirit and all will go well. Shrug off the bad. Nothing can bother you if you refuse to allow it, and this you must do today. A positive attitude will see you through everything, and you will be surprised at how easy it is to get through a crisis when you refuse to accept the negative side of anything.

Take care not to fritter away your time and concern; the conviviality that prevails could tempt you to do so. The strong powers of self-expression and attraction should be used toward the goals you are seeking. To waste them would be a crime, for everything is needed in your drive toward whatever it is you want in life. Apply them in your business, home affairs, and social activities; these will always continue to exist in your scheme of things and must be constantly enhanced.

An appreciation of the arts will stir you to perhaps take in an art show, a play, or the ballet. Do so by all means—it will give you more pleasure today than on most other days. Dress up and invite someone to join you. Enjoy each moment and end the day with a marvelous feeling of contentment.

Number 4 Individual Day

Work will be the order of the day, so don't think about any social activity. You can attend to all those tasks that you just haven't been able to get around to lately. Start the day early and work as late as possible, keeping yourself to a tight schedule. You will have all the ambition and strength you need to do things that are usually put off because of a lack of interest. However, many of these duties are necessary, and since you will have to do them eventually get at them now. All your efforts will enhance your future.

Any work on an organizational basis or that concerns groups or businesses should be successful today, including signing contracts or partnership deals. An intellectual influence is in attendance and will aid you in such duties.

The home, too, comes in for strong vibrations on a 4-Day, so homeowners will have many domestic chores they can attend to. Together, a couple can discuss and lay plans for the future of their children, perhaps decide on a trust fund, school preparations, savings, building, or moving. Anything that requires strength of mind and careful planning would find success today, and it would be wise to take advantage of this power.

A trip to the dentist or the doctor for a general checkup would also be well advised. These are chores we often hate to do and therefore put off, much to our detriment. Make up your mind that today is the day and get the whole family off en masse to their respective doctors. If this is not convenient, at least make appointments for the earliest date you can manage. Health is something one must not neglect. As long as there is no pain, it is too easy to ignore necessary checkups that might uncover a problem of which you were unaware.

Check through your wardrobe and attend to the buttons that must be replaced, the tears to be mended, the cleaning and pressing. Get at the garage or basement—straighten things up. How about your books or budget? Check your checkbook for mistakes or reorganizing. Your household accounts, too, should come in for scrutiny. Have you been spending too much? If so, today is a good day to go through your accounts carefully to weed out all the unnecessary expenditures. Point them out to the family in a practical way, and they will surely assist you in your reorganization. Mismanagement or lack of concern could throw your whole cycle into economic chaos.

Spend money wisely if you must spend it at all. Be economical and count each dollar twice before making a decision to buy something. Save the luxuries for another day.

Number 5 Individual Day

Do not be surprised if appointments you had for today are suddenly broken, for the nature of a 5-Day is change and action. However, if you are aware of this in advance, you will not be too upset, and can accept it nonchalantly and go on to something else. There will surely be some replacement, because things will move in and out of your day rather quickly and, again, unexpectedly. In fact, this in itself may lead you to break an appointment yourself; something more important or more urgent may come along that you feel takes precedence.

Use the interesting vibrations of your 5-Day to get out and about. Variety is the keyword today, and it can be found if you mingle with lots of different people or groups.

Go somewhere you haven't been before, where you can be sure of meeting a new coterie of people; you are bound to find someone very much to your liking among them. Throw caution and habit to the winds and do all, or at least some, of the things you have always wanted to do. Wear something outlandish, try a new sport; anything that is out of the norm for you will give you pleasure and introduce you to avenues of excitement or exploration that you may well be glad you found. Action will have particular appeal for you, so why not try something in which action or speed are an integral part? Of course, you will want to be careful where speed is concerned, but caution should preclude any problems.

Speed also implies hasty reactions or judgments against which you must guard. Don't jump into anything without thinking it out clearly beforehand, especially where either business or your home life is involved. Be cheerful, by all means, but not irresponsible.

Conversation in all its forms will be a major part of the day; speeches, discussions, meetings, and even quarrels are possible. Intelligent or gay discourse is profitable, but the vibration of speed that would actuate arguments is not to your advantage and should be ignored in this case. Any of the arts connected with words is enjoyable today; plays, films, writing, lectures, radio, or television. Make a point of enjoying at least one of these mediums if you can, and take someone with you, if not a group. Since it's a wonderful day for entertaining or being entertained, why not make up a theater party?

Catch up on your correspondence. If you are moved to write a story, play, or poem, follow your impulse, for you have all the right vibrations to make it a success today, If not literarily creative, a note or card to someone you care about would make a good impression.

Number 6 Individual Day

This should be a day of peace and contentment, and you will enjoy it immensely if you just give in to the quiet impulses you will feel. Your home will be so much more important to you today, as will your family. Six is the number of mankind and all your feelings will be thoughtful and generous as you strive to share them with those you love. They will welcome your eagerness to help shoulder their load and appreciate your kind offers to help. Forget about bills and expenses, for on a 6-Day you will not want. Riches won't abound, but surely all you need will be forthcoming, as 6 falls under the protective force of adequate supply. Accept your responsibilities cheerfully and you will find yourself enjoying doing whatever it is you must. No burden seems too heavy when it is lifted with a spirit of joyfulness and determination.

Entertain in your home if possible, for your home will reverberate with your own particular charm and warmth. Since harmony and beauty will be outstanding in your heart on this lovely day, you are apt to make a more concerted effort to establish these qualities in your home, office, or other surroundings—therefore, it's a good day for entertaining. If this cannot be done, get out with others or go to the homes of friends or your extended family. Bring some little gift that speaks of your appreciation of their relationship in your life. You will win hearts and new friends. Whatever bad spell you may have had will be put aside now, and it is good for those you care for to see you in such a happy state of mind. Grudges should be forgotten and an olive branch extended to anyone you have quarreled with. Since you may also have been at fault, your offer will be considered a gracious gesture, and an even stronger relationship can develop because of the respect you gain accordingly.

Give some serious thought to registering for some course of study—education is a strong vibratory power on a 6-Day and this is certainly the day to start the ball rolling. If you can't enroll in a regular course, take heed of everything around you as life itself is an education, and the experiences we acquire are a lesson in themselves if used to our advantage.

Gardening is a study as well as a hobby and can be most enlightening for those who are so inclined. Affection and love are strong within you, so if you are thinking of proposing or accepting a proposal, do it today. Present yourself in the best light possible and watch the stars shine in the eyes of your intended. Good luck.

Number 7 Individual Day

This is the one day in your nine-day cycle when you should really take it easy and be by yourself. Meditation and thoughtfulness are the keynotes of a 7-Day, so use them to your advantage by getting off on your own and thinking through the problems at hand, your present life, and the future you desire. The clarity of thought and resulting decisions will help you sort yourself out and clear the way for the better things in life.

Action is out of the question for the time being; you will be slow of speech and movement, as each step will be well contemplated before you take any at all. This is as it should be today. This thoughtfulness will possibly help you solve some spiritual conflict within yourself, as 7 is the number of religion and spiritualism. Mystic studies, too, are of interest now, and your curiosity about the occult or strange universal ways will lead to exploration of these fields.

Efficiency will be noticeable in your manner, and any new methods that can bring about a more efficient business routine should be either initiated or brought to the attention of someone who has the authority to mandate it. In the home, of course, one can apply this efficiency in many ways to keep things moving easily, cheaply, and more effectively.

Intellect and creativity will come to the fore, and you should use them in whatever way you feel inclined. Any suggestions along these lines will stand you in good stead with either your employer or marital partner. It would be ideal to get away for a quiet day in the country or by the seashore if you can. The seashore is particularly favored on a 7-Day. How about a swim if you can take some time off? Otherwise, cultural affairs would please you, if you can spare only an evening for entertainment. The home and its complex of problems and situations will occupy a bit of your thoughts today and, if you can sit down and discuss them with all concerned, so much the better.

Consider everyone's opinion before forming your own, and try to make decisions that are practical and will please the majority. Analysis is high on the list of powers today and will help you think clearly and intuitively. It can also cause you to be a bit too analytical and perhaps a bit unfair. Criticism never goes down easily, and some may take offense if you are not careful to be diplomatic. A "holier than thou" attitude must also be avoided and you must take care not to offend anyone.

This is not a propitious day for investing in stocks and bonds or other speculative ventures. Think about it, by all means, for your powers of careful consideration will definitely help you make the correct decisions that you can then carry out tomorrow—an 8-Day which is ideal for such things.

Number 8 Individual Day

Do not waste a single minute of this day of material success. Awaken to a day of all good things and get at it with a wonderful attitude of positivity, for this can be the one most financially successful days of your cycle. The number 8 revolves around business and financial matters and bodes well for them if you put your best efforts into them. Determination and newfound energy will be bestowed upon you to give you the power to do so. If you have been working hard on a project, this could well be the day to start accumulating the wealth you have been hoping for.

Expend all your energies toward improving your finances, even if it means spending the day with an employer in order to secure either a salary increase or promotion.

Seek out opportunities and grasp at any offers that come your way. Make a point of seeing people who can help you, and don't hesitate to ask for that position you want. Ask with confidence and courage, and you are bound to either get it now or at least pave the way for it in the near future. Nothing ventured, nothing gained.

Give your affairs serious thought, and see if you have not perhaps been overlooking certain possibilities to either make more money or make what you do have go further. Rearrange the affairs that have not proved successful and start putting those funds into something else that can bring you more profit. Investments would be well favored today, as well as making or taking out a loan if it is to be used to further your success.

In all your dealings you will have to exercise tact, diplomacy, and consideration so you don't step on toes, which could make matters go against you.

Dealing with charities would also be a good idea, for the power of the 8 also revolves around helping others, even if it is only kind advice that will enable someone to better help themself. Put some time into helping with the affairs of charitable groups if you cannot contribute to its coffers.

Intuition will be heightened today, so rely on it to give you the right direction in all you do, especially concentrating on money or business matters. This sounds mercenary, but it really is not. One must take advantage of the right time for everything, as destiny, too, as been prescheduled. So you are merely following instructions from a higher and more omniscient power.

Time for loved ones and time to make the most of your appearance must be found today. Fuss more than usual over both. Should you be visiting someone you care for—a good time to do so—bring some thoughtful little gift to show your affection.

Number 9 Individual Day

Nine is always the signal that you must clean out your house, so to speak, and prepare for a whole new cycle that starts tomorrow with your 1-Day. End the affairs that have not brought you what you wish if they look as though they probably won't. Don't allow such things to clutter up your life and take valuable time and effort—they will not prove fruitful. This goes for people, too. You should find the courage to do so, as well as an honest and noble spirit with which to do it. Rely on it and don't hesitate to do what you must. Unfulfilling situations and people are like leeches that draw the very blood from you, giving nothing in return, and should be avoided at all costs. There are so many things to do and people to meet in the world, but so little time to do everything. This time should be guarded like treasured jewels and not wasted. Therefore, the 9-Day is calculated for just the sort of housecleaning that will leave you free to function more profitably. Do not compromise once you have made up your mind.

Distance comes into prominence too, which could mean you will take a trip, or deal with someone some distance away. Whatever it is, and you will know sometime during the day, do not neglect it. Send off the wires, letters, and other material that are expected of you in this regard. Should a trip materialize, do not question it in any way; just get ready and go. This could be very rewarding for you.

Mysticism and the occult fall under the vibrations of a 9-Day, and you may want to begin studies along those lines, which could be most enlightening. There are many phases to be explored, without devoting a lifetime to it, if there is merely an inkling of interest on your part.

Creativity is another strong vibration of your 9-Day. As a homemaker this could be reflected in an unusual cake, furnishings in the home, or even the garden. Then, too, perhaps it lies in your mental pursuits; but, whatever or wherever, give vent to it, and you will find pleasure.

Anything of a confidential nature should be attended to, with great care taken not to divulge any secrets told to you. Give whatever advice you can, honestly, but do not enter into any sort of deception or be involved in a lie.

Competitive activity is in your favor today, so chances are you won't lose. Why not take advantage of this by participating in some sport or promoting some worthy cause? Charitable work will be appreciated by all concerned and will give you a sense of accomplishment. It is a good way to begin your new cycle and will bring its rewards in time.

Your Triple Cycles

Everything has a beginning, a middle, and an end, as a natural progression. First we set the stage, then we set the machinery into motion, and at the end we collect our reward. Your Specific Year is also divided into three separate stages, consisting of four months each. These three stages are called Triple Cycles. Knowing what to do and when to do it helps you use that year to its greatest advantage.

Things are so much easier when properly planned and executed, and that requires a certain procedure. Nothing is accomplished satisfactorily when left to chance. When you know exactly what lies around the next bend, you can channel all your thoughts and efforts in that direction without suffering the disappointment of striving for goals that cannot be attained during that time. Knowing the power inherent in each cycle and concentrating on using it to its fullest degree spares you the frustration of spinning your wheels.

First Triple Cycle

The first of the three progressions in the year starts on your birthday and lasts for four months. To determine the vibration of this period, you merely compute the vibration of the year of your birth. Example: If your birth date is September 30, 1937, reduce the year by adding 1+9+3+7=20. All the zeros are dropped, so 2 becomes the number of the First Triple Cycle, from September 30 to December 30.

Second Triple Cycle

For the Second Triple Cycle, subtract your Destiny Number from the year of your last birthday and reduce to a single digit. Example: The Destiny Number for the above birth date would be found by adding the month, day and year together: 9+3+0+1+9+3+7=32. 3+2=5. Subtract this 5 from the year of the last birthday, 1996, and you have 1991. 1+9+9+1=20. Drop the zero and you have 2, which is the number of the Second Triple Cycle, from December 30 to May 30.

Third Triple Cycle

The Third Triple Cycle is determined by simply adding together the numbers of the first and second cycles and again reducing the total to a single digit. In this example, you would add 2+2 and the total of 4 would be the number of the Third Triple Cycle, covering the period from May 30 to September 30.

Number 1 Triple Cycle

This is always a very advantageous cycle for everyone, and one should make the very most of it. What you have done previously will start rewarding you during this cycle, but that is no reason to sit back and wait to be flooded with all you have been striving for. Your chances of success are very good now, and you must make every effort to bring all your ideas, methods, or relationships into prominence. Never mind the usual day-by-day routine; you can afford to experiment and take a stab at new things. Fill every hour of every day with some new plan or action. If you have had certain ideas that you have done nothing about, now is the time to instigate promotion of them. Assume the role of leadership, and the powers are with you to make good. As a homemaker, this means you can perhaps start working on plans for that new addition you have been wanting or to take over the leadership in a club or some organization. In any case, you will most certainly be the central figure in your household, so put this authority to good use.

For women, relationships with men are particularly favorable during this cycle. Whether they be friends, beaux, husbands, employers, officials, or members of the family, all of these associations should prove mutually profitable. Therefore women would do well to establish solid grounds for future relationships. The friend you cultivate today could be the beau of tomorrow. Your husband could bring you more joy based on the relationship you embellish during this cycle. It stands to reason, of course, that male employers or associates will be extremely helpful to you now and in the future if you take care to work at it now.

Develop new associates wherever possible. Look into the souls of everyone you meet and see if there are grounds for mutual benefit from the relationship—either in business or a lasting friendship. All are important, not from a mercenary sense but from a realistic one. Good friends are difficult to find and sometimes even harder to maintain, so it does take effort, and the effort expended now will be worthwhile. Go out of your way to put yourself out and it will all come back ten-fold.

Number 2 Triple Cycle

Cooperation and coordination will be the guidelines of these four months. Leadership is not indicated at all, so don't even attempt it. You would do best by letting someone else take the lead. You will be a good right hand to have now, so do your utmost to follow through on any task you have undertaken or been assigned. Collaborate by all means. State your opinion and offer your suggestions, but leave the decisions to others. Be flexible and adaptable.

Should you be in a partnership, let your partner use this cycle to make the decisions, and he or she will be most impressed with your spirit of cooperation. It never hurts to let the other person, whether it be partner or mate, feel as though they are equally in charge. If they make mistakes, your common sense can be of value, but if you should usurp the spot of leadership, things are apt to go quite wrong for you. Why risk it?

Just as the last cycle was favorable to relationships with men, this one is most favorable to women. So defer to the women in your life; make appointments with female business associates, start new romances, new friendships, and the like.

If you have daughters, this would be a good time to pamper them and make them feel like princesses. Show your love and spend time in special projects with them. You will be rewarded by new love, respect, and understanding. A strong bond could develop now that will delight you in future years.

Indulge your imagination and sense of creativity. Whether a tyro or an expert, anything you create can be worth a great deal to you. Whatever your talents or ideas, they should be allowed to run the gamut. Make the time.

Number 3 Triple Cycle

Three, being the symbol of self-expression, will bring great rewards during this period if so used. You will want to take full advantage of this power by devoting all your time to people, preferably large groups of them at once. In fact, the larger the group, the better the influence of the three, since it affects group consciousness most beneficially. This includes clubs or large organizations of any sort, both business and social. Be an active, participating member of these groups—make yourself known and your powers felt. Express yourself fully and clearly. Don't just be there. Let social groups revolve around *you* if possible. Give parties, luncheons, teas, or any other such thing. If this is not convenient, accept all invitations given to you or drop in to see your friends, business associates, or family often.

Business people can have lunch, dinner, or cocktails with colleagues if their tight schedules preclude socializing in any other way, though the more people involved the better. Save the private tête-à-têtes for more quiet cycles. Try, in particular, to be in the company of your superiors, as they are more likely to be impressed with you in a 3-Cycle.

Self-expression calls for a witty, charming, and endearing variety—not the overintellectual and rather dry sort. Save that for a 7-Cycle. Personality, humor, and wit will score many points during this cycle and should take priority. You will be extremely popular and inundated with invitations as a result of the strong influence of the 3-power, if you use it to the fullest.

With all the playing around and socializing that will go on in this cycle, don't get carried away and ignore the financial situation. There may be a tendency to overlook things when you're involved in a social whirl. You could easily fritter away too much money in the course of your social obligations, so be doubly careful. Finances should be very good during this period if you pay enough attention to them.

Number 4 Triple Cycle

After all the gadding about in a 3-Cycle, the 4-Cycle may be a little difficult to settle down to at first; but I'm afraid you will have to do so. As always, 4 denotes hard work and keeping your nose to the grindstone. It means time to build a business or home ties—to build in general. That precludes much social life, but don't worry. You had enough of that for a spell in your last cycle and will have to do it again; you had better stick to work when it is necessary to do so. In any case, the work you do now will pave the way for rewards in the future; so you are merely adding to an account, as it were.

Actually you may have to work harder than usual now. It may get you down at times, but it is all a part of this cycle. You will reap only what you sow, so sow you must. Don't complain about how much effort you are putting into whatever you are doing. It will only tire you more and cannot be avoided in any case, so it is best to do it with the joy and knowledge of the better things that are coming. You will emerge from this cycle a much better and wiser person, which will stand you in good stead in the future. One never exerts effort without learning something from it, and that is the axis on which our world turns. It is not enough to merely learn; you must experience. This experience will stay with you forever, to be taken out whenever it is needed for your advancement. Better to work now and store the experience against the day you might otherwise be dry. You will regret it deeply if you do not.

Your home and business will be the center of your labors during this cycle, and it is a good opportunity to accomplish all you have been meaning to. Laboring for a social group or organization would best be left to a better cycle, perhaps a 2, 3, 5, etc. Now this, oddly enough, does not necessarily mean redecorating the home—there are cycles that are better for creative or decorative activity, such as that would require, but, nevertheless, you will be deeply involved with reorganizing the home activities, maybe putting up preserves, getting the grounds in shape, and that sort of thing. Good, hard, manual labor.

Find time even in your exhaustion and preoccupation to be sympathetic and tolerant of others or you could be a bit of a bore. Put yourself out to listen to the problems of others and give the best counsel you can. It will take you out of yourself and will be greatly appreciated.

Number 5 Triple Cycle

Nothing lasts forever, so, all the hard work of your 4-Cycle is now giving way to a more fruitful and exciting period. Five always denotes change, learning, and experiencing. Open your mind and heart to each of them. Change in itself is not the important thing here; only if it denotes progress is it to your advantage. Keep this all important factor uppermost in your mind. Accepting the element of change that is always present in a 5-Cycle, whether it be in a Life-Path, Personal Year, Personal Month, or here in your 4-Cycle, must be done with equanimity. Again, I repeat, only when it denotes progress and something is learned from it, can it be helpful to you. To change just for the sake of changing without regard to what ways it can be of use in your life will bring on an extremely negative attitude of fickleness, which must definitely be avoided if you arc to find any happiness. Each change of pace should add another dimension to your life; a deeper awareness of people and places, and an understanding of world problems.

Travel could play a major part in this cycle and is to be relished if you have the opportunity to get away. It will mean new faces, new friends, and new experiences—all of which will be invaluable to you. Keep your eyes open for travel opportunities if you are due for your regular holiday leave. It may be that you have to make your own opportunities. In any case, the time is propitious, and you will be feeling a bit of wanderlust to get you started in the right direction. Therefore, work on it and use these vibrations as they were meant to be used. No time could be better than now.

Five is also a number of the bad omen, if one is not careful. Speed is an inherent trait of the 5-Nature as well, so you would do well to take care during this cycle not to hasten in anything you do. That means actions as well as travel. Savor each moment, knowing that one follows after the other in a perfectly natural manner and there is no need to speed up the process. The next moment, city, or relationship may not have as much to offer as the present one; so why not linger as nature intended? Time needs no help from you, so easy does it. Rest assured that all things material are well favored now, and all things dealing with words should be exploited: discussions, writing, speaking, or sales.

Number 6 Triple Cycle

Six is always a warm, loving, and rewarding number in an emotional sense. You will be surrounded by peace, beauty, and culture during this time, since a 6 thrives on these things. You will allow no discordant note to intrude on your desire for harmony.

Six has also come to mean a source of material supply. "Thou shalt not want" applies to those in this 6-Cycle if they make an effort to get whatever they need or want. It will not just drop into their laps, but if they go after it, it will more than likely be forthcoming, especially if they are prepared to share this windfall with others not under the influence. To give is always to receive. We must not question from where it came, but be grateful for the fact that it did. To be selfish with these gifts will tend to dissolve their abundance or efficacy in a short time, so that you will not be able to enjoy them after all. Therefore, take care in how you go after, accept, and use this good fortune, for your own sake.

You will no doubt have a desire to learn or perhaps be in a better position to do so during this period, as learning is extremely well favored now. Take advantage of the opening of the mind and spend as much time as you can absorbing knowledge. Should you not be able to indulge in formal studies of some kind, which you really should make an effort to do, at least try to use your free time studying some subject of importance or interest to you. Read newspapers and magazines with an eye to the more intellectual items. Read books, preferably fact, rather than fiction, whenever you can sneak in a few paragraphs. Make a point of absorbing each thought and storing it away for the time when it will come in handy. Don't merely read words. If you are in business, spend time brushing up on your own and your competitors' methods. This just may be the time when you will see something that can advance you. Be prepared to shoulder responsibility, for that, too, is one of the vibrations of this cycle. Be the tower of strength to all who need it, especially your family. Six is the symbol of humanity, and all efforts in that direction should be expended willingly and lovingly.

Family and home life come to the fore during this period, so enjoy an extra bit of affection or romance. It generally means a change in your romantic life is likely. If married, you will have a very peaceful, loving period. If single, it could mean that this is your best time to get married. In any case, the positive aspects can only bring happiness, if you follow that route exclusively. Ignore arguments or any negative aspects completely and all will be well.

Number 7 Triple Cycle

This is a great period for you to do a bit of mental cleansing, refurbishing, and expanding, because 7 is all introspective and mental. You will want to think hard about everything before you do it. Meditating, just for the opportunity to sit by yourself and enjoy it, will be a great pastime for you.

This is a wonderful time to go over all your past and current affairs in your mind and see where you can eliminate those that are not proving beneficial or enjoyable. This may mean friends, associates, or acquaintances. All will have a bearing on your life and must be reappraised. This being a mental period, you will want to expand your mind and knowledge, perhaps in the study of the mystical, which is usually very interesting in a 7-Cycle. Many creative people in the field of music or invention find this time extremely rewarding for putting their thoughts and ideas to work. Since it is more mental than physical, it will require that you work out all your concepts from an intellectual and practical viewpoint, rather than a physical implementation of them. Leave that to others whom you must guide.

Because you may be more than normally introspective now, there will be a tendency to deliberate too long over certain things that require your decision. Or you will be slow in getting to places or in doing something that is expected of you. This must be guarded against or you will lose out on something of importance to you. Contemplate by all means, but don't overdo the caution in your workday life. Do your meditating when time permits you the seclusion and freedom from other duties.

Communication will implement your work and desires this cycle; so if you can further yourself or a project through personal communication, by all means do so. But limit your personal contacts to small groups for now. You will not be as outgoing and effervescent as you would in a 3- or 5-Cycle.

Spiritualism is also a great influence in 7-Cycles—more so than at any other time. Avoid relationships that have no spiritual basis during this cycle. In other words, romances or partnerships that are sincere and based on honesty and belief in a Higher Power are beneficial. Others are not, so beware of flighty or fickle relationships for now.

Number 8 Triple Cycle

At last, the power of the all-important, all-rewarding 8 is yours. Whatever you wish will automatically be granted during this cycle if you reach out for it. All of this power can be put to good use to attain all you have worked for during the past seven cycles. Each one was a cog in this mighty, forceful wheel of 8.

Business can go exceptionally well now because it is within your power to direct it in whatever way necessary to reap the benefits you desire. Have no fear of this power and do not hesitate to use it, even though you never had the courage to do so previously. Even the shyest and most reticent of people come into their own now. The only deterrent is their reluctance to step up and be heard or to take the steps in the right direction to claim their heart's desire. You will receive nothing if you do not assert yourself and go after what you want. Of course, this does not mean stepping on other people or utilizing improper methods, because the power of the 8 is strong and beneficial only when shared.

Luckily, you will not have to concern yourself with how to decide what you should do or which offers to accept, for discrimination will be an added benefit now. You will somehow know just what is right and what is not, so don't waste any energy in worrying about it. You will quite easily recognize the powers as they are injected into the mainstream of your affairs and will understand fully the use of them. Concern yourself only with what you truly want out of life. Give it much thought, for you will not want to waste this propitious period by vacillating away the time, which will be another seven cycles in returning.

This would be an excellent time to expand your finances, or at least to start the ball rolling in that direction. Certainly investments are most favorable. Stocks should be watched closely, for the chance of a good return now is high. If you intend to sell property or equipment, do it now while it is more likely to fetch a good price. If you are a creative person, show your wares; inventors will sell their patents; artists of any kind, their works.

Whatever you do, strive to be better than anyone else. Expend your best effort, whether you feel it's your position to do so or not. But it must be done so as not to hurt anyone—a position gained by stepping on someone else will not bring you happiness, nor will the money that is forthcoming. Anything gained in an 8-Cycle—or any other cycle for that matter—must be shared with the less fortunate in order to perpetuate your good fortune.

Number 9 Triple Cycle

Now we come to the last of the cycles before starting all over again. For that reason, the 9-Cycle is a combination of both the end of old methods and situations and the beginning of new. By that I mean that you must cull all your affairs and relationships for that which is of no benefit to you. We can only do so much in a lifetime, and it is far easier to attend to those things that will bring happiness and peace if we do not drain our time and efforts with unrewarding tasks. Work that is not really suited to your intellectual or aesthetic senses should be dropped in favor of work that you truly enjoy doing and with which you have an affinity. To continue at a job or in a business that does not satisfy you is to waste all your inherent talent and the resulting destined success. One can never go against destiny and be happy. There is nothing but disappointment and discontent should you do so.

Many people have a strong desire to do one thing, but circumstances force them into another, like going into the family business when they would prefer, deep down, to be an attorney or a doctor. The strong urge is destiny trying to direct them to the right course. It is the only way that is smoothly paved and that will hold all the joys you seek, so it is foolish to deliberately ignore it.

That is why in a 9-Cycle it is important to sort out one's ideas, plans, and goals. If you concentrate only on what you really, truly want and make up your mind to pursue only that, you will find everything you seek. After you sort yourself out, you must start in the next cycle to put your plans in motion.

Don't be unhappy about the ending of any relationships. Remember that you are clearing the way for new ones and that you will find much joy in them if your life isn't cluttered up with obstacles. By all means, retain those friendships, ideas, or methods that have merit. They may not come to fruition yet; but if you feel positive toward them, then they will be fulfilled in proper time. Perhaps something you have been working at needs alteration or reorganization, however, and that's why it hasn't been successful yet. This is the time to give it a lot of thought and do that reorganizing. Then you will realize the rewards of your efforts.

Be positive as you say farewell to all the flotsam and jetsam in your current life, and be ready and willing to start the whole new cycle of events all over again next cycle, which will be a 1-Cycle. Meet the new experiences and challenges with the kind of positivity that is meant to bring you all the joys and contentment of life.

Letter Vibration Chart

The following chart (repeated from page xxiv) is used to convert all the letters in the alphabet to their numerological vibrations. Use it whenever you want to calculate a name's vibration. After several conversions you will know automatically the number value for each letter by heart and won't have to check the chart.

NUMBERS & CORRESPONDING LETTERS								
1	2	3	4	5	6	7	8	9
A	B	C	D	E	F	G	H	I
J	K	L	M	N	O	P	Q	R
S	T	U	V	W	X	Y	Z	

7

Your Name Expression

This is a method providing you with the quickest answers and the most fun. It is a form of instant analysis that allows you to analyze your friends, family, mate, or date very quickly. You need only to master the nine Name Expressions and you've got it made, without even having to know anyone' s birth date.

Got your eye on someone special? Fret not because this method unlocks the door to his or her very secret thoughts and desires, the knowledge of which puts you far out ahead of bothersome competition. And that is a million-dollar key!

There are three different expressions hidden within the letters of your name: that of the vowels, the consonants, and the total of the two. We will take them individually, since they all indicate different phases of the personality.

In calculating the expression of a name, you use the name by which you are best known. Men often use their full name, including a middle initial for business, but are called a nickname by their family and friends. In this case, the business name would reveal ambitions that are applicable to the man's career, and his nickname would reveal desires and personality characteristics of a different nature.

Married women are often said to take on the numerological characteristics of their husbands, and they do in fact take on the vibrations of his surname. However, the vibrations of the name given at birth endow them with the characteristics with which their pre-marriage personality was formed and this, of course, has to be considered.

The only times I have ever found discrepancies in a Name Expression are when parents were uncertain what to name their children until after their birth, causing conflict by denying the child their true vibrations destined by fate.

Vowel Expression—
Your Secret Desires

Vowel expression is your secret weapon when trying to woo that special someone. It reveals thoughts, ambitions, and desires of which a person is often unaware. A little clever calculation can give you the key to make him or her play right into your hands—and what an enviable position that is! Remember, the vowels denote a secret desire and it is just that, a secret. People do not always admit to or want to know them.

Many bachelors give the impression of preferring swingers, yet deep in their hearts they are really looking for a good, old-fashioned girl. Therefore, the lucky woman who takes the time to plumb the depths of his personality has a good chance of stripping him of his bachelorhood.

If it's money you are after, it certainly helps to know the secret thoughts of your employer or other accessible sources so you can intelligently deal with them when asking for a raise or making suggestions.

To reveal these all-important Secret Desires hidden in any name, print the name out on paper exactly as it is used. For your convenience, the number/letter correspondence chart is repeated below. Ascribe to each vowel the number found above it. For example:

```
    5 1             5   6   = 17
  B E A   M C G R E G O R
```

Reduce this by adding 1+7=8. Therefore, 8 is the Vowel Expression you would check in the following sections for analysis of that vibration.

[handwritten: T i N A   A c k e r m a n ⑦ ⑧]
[handwritten: 9 + 1 = 10 ①   5   1]

NUMBERS & CORRESPONDING LETTERS								
1	2	3	4	5	6	7	8	9
A	B	C	D	E	F	G	H	I
J	K	L	M	N	O	P	Q	R
S	T	U	V	W	X	Y	Z	

Number 1 Vowel Vibrancy

One is always the symbol of leadership and therefore, no matter what your other characteristics reflect, you will continually need to give vent to this urge of personally leading or directing every facet of your life. You may not know this is so but, since this vibrancy is inherent in your name, it is the path for you to follow, and you will eventually find that this is the only way in which you can be happy. This may necessitate many changes in all aspects of your life: perhaps your business, personal relationships, location, and manner of dress or speech. Make them without concern and you are bound to be pleased.

You may be unaware of your powers of leadership and may not have used them, but you would surely have then been aware of restlessness or impatience with the methods of those around you—thinking, perhaps subconsciously, that you would do things differently. This, of course, is your soul urge, and until you free it from its repressive bonds you will continue to feel the restlessness.

Leading does not always mean that you must be the top executive in your firm, or even the president of a group, because there are other people to contend with who may not be willing to step down, but it always means that your thoughts and expressions will be of noteworthy value. These thoughts can be channeled properly into the areas of your interest to attain anything you wish. The constancy of valid thoughts and ideas will eventually lead to the position of leadership to which you are entitled, whether it be in business, social affairs, or marriage.

When you function completely on your own you are very strong-willed, courageous, and full of determined ambition. With these powers, nothing can deter you. No one can stand in your way or change your mind, and no effort is too much.

Understandably, these same traits prevent you from functioning at your best when you have to work with or under someone else. There would be constant friction as you strain to assert yourself, knowing that it is not your place. On the occasions when this happens you are adjudged dictatorial and domineering, and relationships suffer, so it is best to steer yourself along unhindered and uncluttered paths to express your ideas and concepts in the best way you know how.

It's senseless to get involved with people or any business that places you in a secondary position, for it will be difficult for you to suppress the strong urge and capacity to lead the way. You just will not feel good in your skin if you have to take orders or kowtow to anyone.

Number 2 Vowel Vibrancy

You have a conciliatory nature that makes you the best sort of friend to have. You are always trying to smooth over bad patches, and your friends come to you for well-taken advice and consolation. You can generally ease situations, no matter how rocky the path seems to be.

You are a friendly soul and love to do all the little things to make other people happy that so many of us don't think of. This is a trait that your friends treasure in you because it is touching to be remembered in these little ways.

Peace and happiness for all is your motto, and you go out of your way to bring this philosophy to the stage of reality. Sometimes this may take its toll on your nerves, but you prefer that to unpleasantness.

Cooperation is another marvelous trait that will aid you throughout life. There is not much that you wouldn't do to be helpful in any way. This usually allows you to be pliable enough not to require much persuasion in any direction. Of course, you have to exercise caution in this regard because you will not want to be led astray, which would not be too difficult. A soft plea with a tear or winning smile will win you over every time.

Always diplomatic and tactful, you rarely say the wrong thing. What a wonderful asset for any position or marriage! It can never be said that you were the instigator in any disagreement. Even if you know you are right and the other is wrong, you won't fight for your point.

You are always on your toes, constantly aware and alert; so little gets by you if you don't wish it to. You generally analyze everything carefully and then try to point out most tactfully where the faults lie, whether it's in a marriage, personal relationship, or business.

Being tardy for anything is just not in your book. You are consistently on time and steady in your relationships—it's not surprising that everyone relies heavily upon you.

Wisdom and kindness are two more of the facts that keep your popularity rating at a high point. This, coupled with your desire for peace and your analytical mind and diplomacy, makes you an excellent judge of character. Surface hostility doesn't throw you off, as you know well enough that people are often hostile out of a sense of fear, and you feel great sympathy for them and make every effort to get them to unwind.

All things beautiful—music, art, and fashion—put you in a peaceful, joyful mood. One day you would enjoy an art show or play and the next a simple day in the country. Things mystical also interest you and may be explored if the mood comes upon you.

Number 3 Vowel Vibrancy

What a happy, friendly soul you are. So pleasant and joyful, you always find the cheerful side of everything. Words are like jewels, to be savored, played with, enjoyed, and stored away for use when something special is needed. You wear words and phrases as one would wear clothes. A good conversation is your greatest joy and expressing yourself is a gift. The words form into colorful, descriptive phrases deep in the recesses of your imaginative mind and flow from you like wine.

Entertaining in your special creative way is one of the pleasures of your life, whether you have one or a hundred guests. In fact, the more the merrier. Friends rarely refuse an invitation unless it's really unavoidable, because your parties are always successful. You have a knack for setting the perfect stage and then inviting all the right types to mingle interestingly and easily. No one feels ill at ease because you see to it that everyone has a wonderful time.

With this talent you have for words, you do get carried away at times and color the truth a bit. Not that you mean to exaggerate—it's just that you can't bear the colorless things in life and enjoy brightening them up to the point where they are tolerable. Being an entertainer at heart, you thrive on the intent expressions on the faces of your audience and feel you should give them their money's worth, and so you add a bit here and there. It's never meant to harm and is certainly not conceit as the word is generally interpreted. When you relate stories of your various feats, you are generally thrilled with your accomplishments and speak of them only because you are so amazed and excited about them. You get carried away in order to share the thrill with your friends so that they may understand the excitement of it all.

Generosity and kindness make you a happy individual when you are able to share whatever you have, and sad when you have nothing to give. If you were wealthy, you would spend all your money on others, buying all the things they have always wanted and could never afford. It would be your greatest pleasure to sit back and enjoy their happiness if it were in your power to bestow these gifts upon others. If not, you would prefer to retreat into your own little world rather than face the fact that you cannot give to the point you would like. Unfortunately some will assume this means that you are moody and selfish. Nothing could be further from the truth.

Number 4 Vowel Vibrancy

A great perfectionist, you cannot bear to leave anything half finished. You will stick to any task until it is completed to your satisfaction, no matter how long it takes to do so. You are very orderly, never leaving anything lying about or messy. Everything has its proper place and you see to it that that is where it goes. As an employee, you are an asset because of this trait. Your employer can always be sure that a job will be done in the best possible way without having to stand over you to direct you. As a parent, this will carry over in keeping up an orderly home and in raising well-mannered children. It can never be said of you that you are lazy or lackadaisical. You won't leave whatever you are doing for some spontaneous flight of fancy—whether your own or anyone else's.

You always seek the most practical way in anything you do, and this practical nature leads to the establishment of definite routine procedures so that things can be accomplished to your satisfaction. The line must be drawn clearly and the path fully lighted for you to travel upon it.

Honesty and sincerity play a big part in your life, and you demand these qualities in others. What you say you mean, and what you promise you fulfill, no matter how difficult. It is only right that those around you abide by these standards, since you give them the benefits of these wonderful traits.

Wastefulness is sinful in your book, and you cannot abide it in anyone. You work hard for what you have and feel it should be fully appreciated; therefore, you cannot waste it.

Trivialities and silly arguments also annoy you. You would prefer to help people work out their problems or avoid them completely, rather than listen to petty disagreements. Yet, in your most negative nature, you can be very argumentative. This negativity could also bring out the gossiping and even deceitful side of you if you do not take care to suppress it. Negatively, you could also become caustic and make silly blunders that will hurt people when you least intend to.

In your positive nature, you are most ethical and conscientious, which in itself would help you to put down the negative aspects of your character. Normally, you are quite fearless and certainly should not let anything of a detrimental nature upset your equilibrium. You are astute enough to ferret it out long before it can undermine you or your efforts.

Number 5 Vowel Vibrancy

Versatility, curiosity, and constant change are the keynotes of your life. The world is too big and too full of wondrous adventures for you to be satisfied in one place or one relationship for very long. Where others concern themselves with the best methods to make the monthly budget stretch and plan where they might go on the next two-week vacation, your mind is full of gay, romantic thoughts and plans. You could easily sail around the world without a thought of getting ahead in business. As a woman, you would tire quickly of the day-to-day routine of married life and, though you could probably discipline yourself sufficiently to control your constant flights of fancy and make a good home, you would always dream of what could have been.

You can only be enthusiastic about a new venture if it doesn't require you to be involved with all the necessary minor and practical details and schedules. If someone else takes that unpleasant and boring chore off your hands, you will reward them greatly by the marvelous curiosity and enthusiasm you exude with every new discovery, making the trip so much more enjoyable and memorable. However, to thoroughly enjoy the trip or holiday yourself, you would need a transitory affair. Romance is your life, and you could no more do without it than air.

Bonds of any kind are not for you. You must be free to think, feel, and do exactly as you like, when you like. In marriage you can be an excellent and exciting partner as well as a faithful one if the matrimonial bonds are invisible and strictly of your own choice.

Your friendship is one to be treasured because it will never be of the humdrum variety. Others must concentrate on business and family affairs and therefore enjoy hearing in a vicarious way of your adventures into every nook and cranny of life and the universe.

Cleverness and wit combined with a knack for good common sense always see you through, and because you know you can always get by, you never worry too much about building a career or life in the normal sense. You will follow the rainbow forever and, strangely enough, you will no doubt find it time and time again.

Large crowds, with clever, interesting people, are your delight and you take every opportunity to meet new groups, as long as everything keeps rolling and never bogs down. When it does, you are restless and get bored quickly. You prefer ever-changing, ever-moving situations, and love speed and motion.

People are completely captivated with you and find you a brisk and alert conversationalist. You are generally frank and always diplomatic, but your negative nature can make you far too temperamental, egotistical, and impulsive to bring you the happiness you will surely find if you don't allow it to assert its powers.

Number 6 Vowel Vibrancy

Of all the nine Vowel Vibrancies, the 6 would probably have to be awarded the honor of expressing the most humanitarian instincts. You live for the pleasure of doing for others and will do everything in your power to bring happiness to as many people as you can reach.

You can sympathize with the lowliest of human beings and tolerate the worst situations because you believe that there is good in everyone. You believe that the meanness some people project is only because they themselves are so miserable they cannot help themselves. Love is the keynote of your life and you can love many people, expressing the best in you and in turn bringing out their best.

However, this tendency to help everyone and understand even that which is sometimes beyond understanding, often puts you in a very depressed mood. You should try not to get in too deeply so you can extricate yourself when you find this depression coming on, or people will take unfair advantage of you. You often feel the problems of the world are waiting for you alone to solve and, if it were at all in your power to do so, you would certainly try.

Beauty and harmonious environs are as necessary to you as the air you breathe. You have artistic leanings and would like to make a name for yourself in some artistic field. Wherever you live, it is bound to be beautiful, peaceful, and charming, as an extension of your need to live as such; but it entrances all those who are privileged to share it with you, making your home a joyous place to be for one and all. Problems and worries disappear in this setting.

The unjust or tawdry have no place in your life. Not only can you not make a place for them, even in the smallest way, but you refuse to accept that anything can be of this nature. If you cannot make all things lovely, you have to reject them completely rather than let their shabbiness dim the luster of your philosophy.

The very young and the very old will generally be the delighted recipients of your warm affection, as you express your love most easily with them. The sympathy you feel for old or infirm unfortunates manifests itself in unselfish devotion. You cannot bear to see them rejected or ignored and give unstintingly of yourself to make them happy and comfortable.

Children adore you because you are innocent and sincere when dealing with them. No tricks for you, just love and concern. You have compassion for them in all their little problems. Popularity and adoration are yours without effort, because you are always infectiously enthusiastic, active, and bright. The scene you grace is charged with warmth and gaiety, wherever it may be.

Number 7 Vowel Vibrancy

The secrets of the universe, yet undiscovered, hold a deep attraction for you. You will probe and seek the answers to the mystical questions that surround the study of the occult, and keep these answers to yourself. You will delve quietly but constantly, first into one subject and then another, until you learn all you can about each, storing this knowledge away for future use. You have no need in particular to brag about your discoveries or inculcate your friends with the mystic phenomena that entrances you. It is sufficient for you alone to understand and believe.

You study people quietly, always analyzing. Again, you have no need to divulge your impressions. You possess great powers of insight and understanding and can generally size up a person very quickly, usually correctly.

Selfishness is not one of your bad characteristics, and you can most often be counted on to give of yourself or your possessions when convinced it is for a good cause. Your soul's urge is for courage, intelligence, and spiritual bravery, on which you put the highest value for yourself as well as for others around you. You greatly admire anyone with these traits and are quickly attracted by such people, entering into satisfying and long-lasting relationships.

Dignity is also important to you, and it is unlikely that you could have a serious romantic relationship with anyone lacking this necessary trait. You feel that all life should be dignified, even in its squalor.

You are authoritative whenever need be, drawing on that wonderful store of knowledge to which you keep adding each little tidbit you discover. Then you are specific in your statements, backing them up with facts that can be checked and understood by anyone in doubt.

Idealistic, you wish you could change whatever needs changing in our world of turmoil, but realize the danger in proselytizing. Therefore, you confine your efforts to improving your own way of life and that of those close to you, in whatever way they allow it.

To permit your negative side to come to the fore would be to reverse the good you can do for yourself. You would become egotistical and complaining. Your usual knack for intelligent conversation would be replaced with an argumentativeness that would undo all the good impressions you might have established. Instead of being friendly you would become aloof and uninterested in people. Needless to say, you must eschew negativity in order to allow the positive side of your nature to work toward the goals you have set for yourself.

Number 8 Vowel Vibrancy

Success in your particular field of endeavor is your strongest ambition. Working for a salary to pay your bills is not for you. You must attain the heights of fame, power, and fortune before you feel you can be satisfied. It is your belief that only these three goals will bring you what you desire in life, which is the very best of everything. Nothing can be second best, only top quality will do, no matter what it may be. Rather than purchase an automobile that is practical for you or your family, you would prefer to buy one that is outstanding in style and prestige. And so it goes with everything in your life.

Destiny is on your side, however, and can provide you with whatever it is you want, because it has bestowed upon you the powers of great sales ability and the persuasion needed to indoctrinate those who are necessary to you in your ambitions. You can convince anyone of your beliefs and methods and can properly merchandise any product or idea to successfully reap the rewards you desire. You rest right on the dividing line between benevolence and its destructive opposite, malevolence. You must be extremely careful to use your wonderful powers only for good or you will destroy your own empire. Use your position and wealth to help the less fortunate and you will go on to dizzying heights of glory and success.

As a philanthropist you will find that the more you give, the more you receive, and your coffers will be refilled constantly. Selfishness will only reward you with depression and loneliness. Your soul's urge is to understand the more advanced planes of life and to move ahead in these areas; therefore, you should develop great spiritual power, as you progress along these lines. With your wonderful powers of persuasion this can lead to the enlightenment of so many who are not possessed of the tenacity or understanding it takes to ferret out these truths and find serenity.

You can lead them to this spiritual contentment and know a kind of happiness that few people ever attain—that of truly understanding and helping others to find a joy that would not be possible without your help. You are analytical by nature and yet tactful when making your analysis known. Wisdom and alertness allow you to anticipate in advance various thoughts or methods. Therefore, you can be right on top of a situation and produce results. This may be in personal relationships such as marriage, as well as in business. Anticipating your mate's wishes or moods helps you to avoid unpleasantness, which you cannot abide.

The negative side of an 8-Vibrancy can bring out the side of you that makes you most unpleasant. You could tend toward being too contradictory or impatient with others and even deceptive, all of which are circumnavigated if you permit your positive vibrancy to rule.

Number 9 Vowel Vibrancy

The finer things in life are your great joy. What you do not create yourself, you can enjoy in others. Your vision of the world and all that life holds is one of immense beauty—almost saintly in its concept. You continually dream great dreams of this loveliness and happiness, and wish that you could wave a wand and bestow upon every living soul these same visions.

When the beauteous aura surrounding your life is torn, and the ugly and miserable aspects of true life are revealed, you are repulsed to the point of pain. You desire only beauty and perfection, and this deviation from your dream is incomprehensible.

If it were in your power to do so, you would help each individual to attain some great measure of success and artistic fulfillment in order to reverse the ugliness and misery that you cannot abide. It is to your credit that this would be done for the betterment of the universe in general and not just to satisfy a whim.

Your greatest joy comes from doing good works that will profit mankind. Material rewards or possessions are not all that important, and you would be much happier with spiritual rewards. Knowledge of metaphysics or psychic phenomena are to you what jewels would be to others.

Esthetic thoughts and ideas give you wonderful inspiration, which you generally manifest in an artistic way. You would enjoy using this artistic sense, in whatever form it is presented, to paint over the drabness of the world and convert it to shiny brightness. This could be in a physical sense or a spiritual one.

Always congenial and sociable, there are times when you can be dazzling, if the company is right. You have a level head on your shoulders and can usually think things out clearly; but you can also be gay and lighthearted at times, which is most charming and captivates your companions.

When you endeavor to beautify either a home, office, or wardrobe, it is done not only from a style sense but a spiritual one as well. Your home, though beautiful in its furnishings and colors, must also reflect a sense of serenity and charm. People must want to come to your home because they feel so peaceful there, and you plan with this in mind.

As a decorator or designer you could not design for lines and style alone but to frame the personality of the person involved. The rest would be secondary. With your artistic and esthetic combination, it is always certain that the correct effect will be achieved.

Negatively, you could be cynical and cowardly. Your usual esthetic manifestations would be replaced by vulgarity and shriek with disharmony. You would lose your drive and become slow and snail-like in manner. Avoid these traits by developing only the positive side of your beautiful nature.

𝓔

Consonant Expression:
The Real You

We all respond to various groups or individuals. Jealousy, love, hate, envy, disrespect, and antagonism are all traits that can be successfully suppressed within the company of certain people and yet clearly evident in the company of others.

Very much like colors that change to different shades when you add even the slightest amount of a different hue, your personality takes on the shading of the people you are with. If they are solemn, your tendency would be to act reserved and quiet. If they are gay you would most likely add a cheery note to your voice and general attitude. So you can see where the true personality often gets lost among the many variations and shadings.

How can you tell what someone's true personality is, without sham or affectation? Merely add up the number value of the consonants in their name and you can be very sure of your ground, for the consonant vibration reveals the true personality of someone when they are truly at ease and completely themselves. Though the vowel vibration may be a secret, the consonants show what you express openly. To find this vibration, print the name in full. Ascribe to each consonant the number you find above it in the chart that follows.

NUMBERS & CORRESPONDING LETTERS								
1	2	3	4	5	6	7	8	9
A	B	C	D	E	F	G	H	I
J	K	L	M	N	O	P	Q	R
S	T	U	V	W	X	Y	Z	

Example: C Y N T H I A P I E R R E
         3 7 5 2 8   7   9 9   = 50
So the Consonant Expression is 5.

Number 1 Consonant Vibration

Your strong willpower is one of the dominant characteristics of your personality. This, combined with another strong factor, your ambition, keeps you going on to newer fields to find what it is you seek.

You must always have a worthy goal if you are to put the time and effort into anything at all. When there is one, you can throw your whole being into a project and generate tremendous enthusiasm and excitement. You must know exactly where you are going and how you will get there; a plan is drawn and you will pursue it relentlessly.

When no clear goal or direction is drawn, you have no interest at all. When you take up a project for your very own, it is almost certain to be a success because you will drive yourself until it is. Your vanity is also a factor here. You would hate to be unsuccessful in anything or to leave things at loose ends—a good trait when properly employed.

Often your passionate nature overrules the wisdom of your mind, and this can at times cause you great heartache. It would be wise to blend the two and intelligently analyze a situation or relationship before letting yourself go completely. This blend of the best of both your heart and mind can be exceptionally rewarding if you only give it a chance.

Your passion can be an asset if you use it in its finer sense and don't inflict it on others who would prefer a more reserved nature. In romance it can be a hindrance if your mate is the quiet, conservative type. Refine it by using its strength and devotion and loyalty instead of engaging in heated arguments and wild proclamations of undying love.

Avoid the domineering aspects of your ambitious drive. To you the aims of a relationship or project may be clearly defined as having to follow certain lines, but to someone else they may not be the same, and your strong insistence will be misunderstood easily.

You like to have everything your own way, but do not see this as an expression of selfishness. You can always find ways of justifying every action or desire as a result.

This expression is a particularly difficult one for a woman if it is practiced in its negative sense, so great care must be taken to use only the positive power of the number 1, which also is great in strength.

With the ambition, drive, and willpower of such a person as you, the finest ideals can be realized and the highest of goals reached. Use them to guide the work of those you live or work with if they have a weaker drive than yours, but suggest and demonstrate rather than demand and dictate.

Number 2 Consonant Vibration

Charm is the means by which you gather to you all that you wish. You have no need for demands or currying favor—your charm so intrigues all around you that it is their pleasure to ply you with all the things for which you express a desire. For this reason you are also a welcome guest at any party. It is known that with you in attendance a host can rest easy, knowing that you will make friends quickly and easily and put the more reticent or reserved guests at ease.

You like to fantasize and then bring your dreams to life. You build upon these dreams, never thinking in terms of an unattainable goal. Your rationalization is that if you can visualize it in your mind, then surely it must be true.

You believe that there are certain rules by which we must live and, if we follow them to the best of our ability, we will be greatly rewarded. If we break these rules, we will have to pay the price. This is your way of thinking, and you live your life in as exemplary a manner as you find possible. You have no patience with those who abuse these rules or who force their way of life on others.

As a mother you will easily be able to express the necessity for the Golden Rule to your children, inasmuch as you live it to the letter. To see is to believe, and to believe is divine. You surround yourself with this fairness and, again, this is to the benefit of your children.

As an employer these traits add to your position, because those who work under or with you can always be assured of an honest judgment in all they do. They will be justly rewarded for a job well done.

This natural desire to help all with whom you come in contact is just a part of an overall generosity and expression of the good you feel inside. But allow these same instincts in relationship to your own situation in life as well. To do all that is good and kind can make your life an everlasting happy one.

This reminder is necessary because there is a negativity in your number 2 that can incite you to anger and cause you to undo all the good you have done if you don't get your way.

Resist the impulse to connive if things do not go your way. If it isn't worth acquiring in an honest and open sense, attaining it by sneaky or foul means is not going to bring you happiness. The positive side of your vibration could never allow you to enjoy anything you are not proud of acquiring. Your conscience would eventually destroy you.

To follow the positive power you have inherited is to assure yourself of an honest, well-earned, and much-appreciated station in life. You will be a shining example to all.

Number 3 Consonant Vibration

You have no fear of what the future may bring, for you believe that only what is good and right will come to you. Therefore, any unhappiness that befalls you can be endured with the understanding that it will pass and be replaced by better events. Positive thinking is your motto and you live it to the hilt. Your belief in the future and all things right makes you understand that whatever may happen, your true destiny was foreordained and nothing can change this.

You cannot abide people who are constantly complaining of bad luck or who rely on lucky talismans for the good things in life. To you this is unnecessary, because no talisman can change circumstances and to believe in that is the only luck one needs.

Your drive for perfection includes your manner of dress and all your environs. You are not demanding in an offensive way and would more than likely be very charming when asking for something to be done the way you like it rather than to be cold and officious.

You feel self-expression is most important in your life and would not hesitate to express your every desire, mood, or approval of anything. When you are happy, the whole world knows it and is benefitted by your mood.

Words and the tone in which they are spoken are, in your opinion, the measure of the person. You would be very cautious in choosing just the right thing to say on every occasion. You believe words and tone signify a level of culture; the literary arts and those associated with the arts are a source of great pleasure for you.

The number 3 is also the number of a great personality. Because of the self-expression inherent in you, a vibrant personality comes quite naturally to the fore without any effort on your part. People are regenerated when in your company and prefer you to any other guest. Always charming and affable, not to mention intelligent, a party usually revolves around you.

Negatively, you may follow the path of weakness, giving in whenever there is an argument or disagreement because you haven't the faith in yourself necessary to defend your rights or opinions.

Self-pity could so envelop you that you do nothing but feel sorry for yourself and the bad luck that you have had in life. You may feel it is just too much trouble to try to correct what is wrong and see the lighter side of things. Nothing is that bad, so this negativity must not be indulged. Your positive vibration brings you the happiness and contentment you desire and should be paramount at all times.

Number 4 Consonant Vibration

A very sturdy, self-reliant soul is one blessed with the power of the 4-vibration. You really don't need anyone else for help or entertainment. Your own company is the best as far as you are concerned, and you are not one to feel the need of constant company or to fear being alone.

Being very well balanced and stable, it is not unusual for your friends to seek your help when they are in trouble. They know you are a tower of strength—if anyone can come to their aid, it is you—and you always do.

Whatever talent or ability you might have, no matter in what field it may be, you use it to its fullest extent and always for the good. You would consider using your talent frivolously to be sinful indeed. Therefore, you generally attain the goals you aim for by positive and constant effort.

The number 4 always stands for hard and devoted labor, but it also signifies that whatever one sows, one reaps. In your case, you sow only the best and will reap only the best, because you cannot sow sickly or weak-minded seeds. Everything you endeavor to do is of the highest merit, at least to you. You could not allow yourself to be involved in anything shoddy or distasteful, if you know it to be beforehand. Unfortunately, should someone deceive you, and enlist your help—which you are always so willing to give—in a project of an unsavory nature, you would no doubt make it a great success. If you were to find out later that it was of such a nature, it would indeed sicken you to be involved.

Remember that the number 4 generally calls for only a partial harvest, and you are not to worry if all your desires are not fulfilled. Be grateful for the fact that you are at least guaranteed the partial harvest, while others are not always so fortunate. Your effort will never be wasted and will always reap rewards.

Beware of always seeing the dark side of things and ferreting out the hardships of life or the projects in which you involve yourself. Your negative side may act as an omen of despair if you allow it to get the upper hand, so you must never permit it to do so.

When controlled by negativity, you tend toward being very difficult to work with, driving your friends or family beyond their endurance. Thus you incur their animosity, which will make you sad because you will be unaware that you are being so hard on them.

Permit your positive destiny to rule your life and you cannot go wrong. You have so much to offer and your world revolves around your contributions.

Number 5 Consonant Vibration

A happy-go-lucky sort, you fly along the path of life with a song in your heart and joy in everything you do. You could not care less about what is to happen tomorrow, for each day is a delightful adventure that you seek with every breath you take. Always happy and carefree, you find pleasure in the darkest corners of the world and can always turn them topsy-turvy until you find the bright side.

As a magical dreamer, you can envision beautiful fantasies and, since they are real in your mind, you will set out in search of them, whatever they are or wherever they might be. Never mind building for a future, you say, because today is to be lived to the fullest and tomorrow will take care of itself. Therefore, you are not always the most stable of employees or marital partners. Whenever you awake to a beautiful day, you are ready to hop the nearest plane, train, or mule to some romantic spot in the world.

Your imagination never allows you to cast your eyes downward to firm ground and security. You prefer to look to the clouds and the universe that contains so many magical secrets crying out for exploration. All things mystical intrigue you. You could easily become a sorcerer for the sheer thrill of unveiling the infinite secrets of life. Your friends may think you irresponsible and a bit mad for traipsing off whenever the urge strikes you, or for not building some sort of secure future for yourself. This is mainly because few people can think like someone with a 5-Vibration, and therefore they cannot understand you.

You have great powers and they should be used to advantage rather than frittered away. If you travel as your wanderlust dictates, make full use of the experiences and the knowledge to be gained, so that you can put them to good use at another time.

Your great interest in everything will always stand you in good stead, inasmuch as that knowledge allows you to work in many fields and gives you a well-rounded background. With this foundation, you will find that through the barter system you can pretty much go where you like. Perhaps you might write travel features in exchange for being able to travel where you wish, thus paying in kind. You will always find a way, of that there is little doubt, but you will be so much the better for seeing the world and relaying your experiences to the less fortunate or carefree of spirit. Concentrate on using every bit of talent and knowledge you have been endowed with and mold it into something of value, so that you can always afford to indulge your fancies.

You must make a supreme effort to avoid being fickle and frittering away your energies and talents. Depression, too, is a constant threat and you truly have to strive to keep yourself from giving in to it.

Number 6 Consonant Vibration

Peace and contentment are your greatest desires, and you easily find them because you live a peaceful life. You don't care for the busy, humdrum activity of exciting places and much prefer a quiet spot somewhere where you can meditate and warm yourself with all the good things you have been given. You know that your desires will be fulfilled if you just concentrate hard enough on what it is you want and believe that if it is good you will have it. For this reason, you mull over anything you may wish for and decide whether or not it is a worthy desire; if you find it so, you put your mind to it and it appears. This faith sustains you in all things throughout life.

There is never any great drive to attain what you desire; you just steadily work toward your aims, knowing that wishing alone is not sufficient. In this way you keep your environment one of peace and harmony, rather than the feverish, tense atmosphere that generally prevails in the case of others when determined to attain certain goals. Your way is far superior, of course, because you enjoy every step of the way and appreciate things so much more.

You give of yourself constantly, knowing that what you do for others, they will do for you. Good will is priceless, and costs you nothing to give, and you spread it wherever you can. It is the one thing you possess that continually perpetuates itself; therefore, it never diminishes in supply. At times, when things go wrong, you draw upon a great source of your faith, knowing that all will be well soon. You do not wallow in self-pity, but rather get on with it.

A comfortable and charming environment is preferable to a 6-Consonant Vibration, rather than one that is so luxurious and elegant you don't feel at ease. You have no need to keep up with your friends and neighbors financially and enjoy whatever you manage to acquire, whether it be a precious antique or a pretty little accessory that is quite inexpensive.

Your home would be bathed in joy, contentment and charm, one that anyone could step into and relax. No need to take off your shoes to go into your home or tread lightly lest you disturb something. Comfort and contentment are too important to you to worry about those things, and that's why your friends always enjoy a gathering at your home. You put everyone at ease, and a good time is had by all.

Number 7 Consonant Vibration

Very little ever really surprises you, for you are always prepared for anything and take it quite easily in your stride— a good trait to have in this hectic world of ours. When all others are in a state of panic, you always manage to keep your head and think sensibly; you are just the person to handle emergencies.

You are also quite happy in your own company and don't need people around you. In fact, you rather enjoy your solitude because you relax completely and take the time and care to sort out all your affairs and then bask in the ease of it all. Therefore, loneliness never assails you, and you don't seek crowds. You can stand well on your own two feet and do not require the agreement of others in order for you to do something you would like to do. You simply go ahead on your own.

You are intelligent, and this sees you through whenever you are in doubt about some action you are contemplating. There is no passionate emotion involved in making your decisions, just quiet contemplation and intelligence. Should something go wrong, you will not belabor the subject but set about correcting what you care to and ignore what is not all that important.

When wrong, you don't try to cover up your errors because you can see why they are incorrect and learn from them. You know that we learn through mistakes and can get something useful from them; so you feel you have gained a bit more knowledge and experience to use positively another time. You are not one to cry over spilled milk.

The happiness of others is paramount to you, and you are moved to action by the plight of those less fortunate. Peace on earth is your main concern, and you would sacrifice anything if you could bring it about. Since you cannot wave a wand and grant a miracle, you do whatever you can to extend the word of peace and work for it whenever the opportunity presents itself.

The sorry state of the world saddens and angers you. You do not hold with the methods or carnage of war. Where others simply disassociate themselves from poverty, crime, and suffering unless they are personally affected by it, you concern yourself with the plight of everyone. Your faith sustains you, and you will rely on it for the strength you need to overcome any adversity and try to instill it in others to help them bear their own burdens.

Number 8 Consonant Vibration

The number 8 is a very powerful one, and you are blessed with all its infinite powers to help you attain all you desire. It is obvious in your thinking as well as in your deeds. You aren't afraid of any type of business because you know that you have the power to make a go of anything. If you are offered a good business proposition in a field with which you are not familiar, you will jolly well make a point of learning all there is to know in order to make a profitable venture. Most likely, it will be with you at the helm.

You don't bemoan your fate when left alone because you can always make that time pay off. This might be when you create new ideas or methods or perhaps improve your mind. Whatever it is, the time will be well spent and not squandered.

Problems are a great challenge to people with the 8-Vibration because they love to take them apart to see what has gone wrong and then reconstruct the matter, using their own techniques to overcome the so-called difficulty—although, to them, it is not a difficulty.

Others may go to pieces when faced with upsets or adversity, but not so an 8-Vibration. They rather welcome the opportunity to wrestle with them if only to prove to themselves that they have the intelligence and power to conquer. It is very much a game of skill with them, and they enjoy it thoroughly.

You think and plan in a very grand manner—nothing small about you! All of your ideas or schemes take on an air of glorious magnitude. Responsibility doesn't frighten you either and, since your schemes are so grandiose, it is usually quite convenient to implement them from a top executive position. That is what you shoot for. Though the position may go hand-in-hand with the concomitant worries and decisions, you prefer to have it that way so that you will have the right to say "yes" or "no."

Your work generally rewards you with material gains—always in a grand manner. Whatever you have is the best you can afford. With your mind constantly set in the direction of fame, power, and fortune, it would be hard not to realize your aspirations.

Number 9 Consonant Vibration

Justice and truth are the foundation upon which you not only build your own life but what you expect of your family and friends as well. You won't brook any deviation of this rule—white lies are just plain lies to you, and you see no need for tolerating such evasiveness.

You can accept almost any weakness in your friends if they can be honest with you. But you will try to help those possessing negative qualities because you feel life is wasted if it is not used constructively. If one has no use for constructive help and ignores any means by which they could better themselves if they wished to, you feel that person is not worth bothering with. Should they make an effort, you will do all you can to help.

Honesty is the keynote in all you do or think. You express this wonderful trait throughout your life, and it is the basis of all your ambition. Before you do or say anything at all, it must ring true with your conscience so that you can forge ahead with great inspiration. Intuitively, you do just the right thing because you cannot stand imperfection. You do not rest until you have achieved this perfection because your conscience would bother you if it did.

You are intelligent, sincere, vibrant, and creative—necessary ingredients for a rich, full, and satisfying existence. Emotionally you require a well-balanced variation. You enjoy people who have something to give rather then insignificant individuals who never have an interesting thought and cannot carry on an enlightening conversation.

You enjoy being in the spotlight but you prefer to share it with others who can build onto what you believe and open doors to new experiences. Material things are not as important to you as fame and respect. It would please you greatly to reach the plateau of fame in some artistic field or as an intellectual.

Nine is the number of universality and 9s are often possessed of some great message for the world that can help us all. As an idealist you will make every effort to help right the wrongs of the universe. Your efforts can never be confined to just one person, group, or nation because of your universal awareness. This applies to your surroundings as well, and you are much happier in large cities with much to offer. If possible, you will travel the globe and absorb all the culture that abounds in every one of the four corners of our world.

Total Name Expression

By adding together the number value of both your vowels and consonants you find the Total Expression of your entire name. This indicates the direction in which you should find your success and happiness. It combines your innermost desires with the outward projection of your total personality and talents, and therefore paints a true picture of your personality.

If you have not yet done so, print your name in full and ascribe to each letter the number value given for it in the chart below. There is no need to separate the vowels and consonants for the Total Expression—just add them all together and reduce the total to a single digit. (For your convenience, the number/letter correspondence chart is repeated at the bottom of page 148.)

Example: R O S E   P A L A Y
          9 6 1 5   7 1 3 1 7 = 40

All zeros are dropped, so the Total Name Expression is 4. See the description of number 4 in the following pages.

Number 1 Name Expression

Number 1 is the symbol of leadership; you blaze the trail and help others to find it. Courage distinguishes you. Although you rebel at commands, you can be responsive to persuasion. Always original, you have a style and a mind of your own. You are a good judge of character, and, on the rare occasions that you misjudge, want to be careful that you're not taken in by those not in tune with your vibration.

Once you decide upon your goal, never waver in your pursuit or you may have to begin all over again. Laziness would be a serious hindrance to you. You are ever-active and productive.

You can afford to live each day to the fullest without having to worry too much about the week to come, as long as you are aware of the fact that your creative mind will find solutions for every problem. But this must not be used

NUMBERS & CORRESPONDING LETTERS								
1	2	3	4	5	6	7	8	9
A	B	C	D	E	F	G	H	I
J	K	L	M	N	O	P	Q	R
S	T	U	V	W	X	Y	Z	

as an excuse for recklessness; that can be your undoing. Take care to listen and learn. Your creativity will keep you forever young, always projecting new ideas to take you into new areas. Anticipation is the clue to your emotional and material happiness; always anticipating the trends, needs, and reactions of people and business allows you to be one jump ahead.

Should you fail to live up to your best Name Expression, you will instead show traits of aggression, selfishness, and haughty conceit, even becoming dictatorial. This can be avoided by remembering that you have the power to do great things without having to bow to precedent or tradition.

Individuality is the cloak you will wear throughout your life, and you believe that all humanity should have the right to express itself freely as well. Every day you will come up against situations in which you will have to stand alone and make your own decisions, not only for yourself but for those who do not have the power of individualism or leadership that has been bestowed upon you. Wear it well and use its power for the good of all humanity.

Number 2 Name Expression

You always see both sides of any situation and can therefore be the perfect helpmate, business partner, or employee. Cooperation is the keynote of your success. Your diplomacy enables you to travel every stratum of society, and you are well liked wherever that may be.

Peace is your great mission in life and your inclination is to try to smooth the way for those who are less capable than you. Your understanding and sensitivity to people's problems, coupled with your intuitive insight, often cast you in the role of peacemaker and analyst.

You are known to be sincere and tactful, so your opinions are accepted quite happily and gratefully. This pleases you because the good will of others is essential to your happiness and can be earned by always trying to see the good side of those around you, no matter how difficult.

As the supreme organizer you can meet your highest goals by making every moment count. Organize your thoughts to coordinate with your goals and never lose sight of them. A good sense of humor comes naturally to a 2-Name Expression, provided he or she doesn't take life too seriously. Being analytical by nature, you still guard against being too unpleasantly critical. You try not to analyze unless you can offer a constructive remedy in a friendly, kindly, or even humorous manner.

When you allow the negative side of your expression to rule, you act conceited and hypocritical, causing people to exploit you to your detriment. Then you wallow in self-pity and fail to analyze your own motives clearly. Another pitfall to beware of is becoming too servile, which is possible in your desire for peace at any price.

The cooperative spirit is one of your finer assets. You enjoy introducing people to new groups or activities and helping them in general to improve their lot in life. Your expressed and deeply felt sympathy and goodwill toward all you come in contact with will bring you continual happiness, and has earned you the reputation of being genuine and sincere. Unhappiness will only enter your life if you allow dissension to interfere with your usual good humor and sensitivity.

Number 3 Name Expression

Through the use of words, you fulfill your Name Expression and work out the problems of life. A vivid imagination and artistic talents bring forth brilliant concepts. This allows you to see all the beauty in life and bring it to others as well. Only in the constant giving of yourself do you really find happiness, for experience is your teacher and service to others your joyous heritage.

Friendship is essential to you. You fully enjoy the social whirl, but it isn't always a satisfying fulfillment of your eager anticipation.

A 3-Name Expression indicates you are a bit too generous or sympathetic, which depletes your stamina and funds, and often puts you in a difficult situation in which friends pull you apart.

Your imagination allows you to find the drama in everything, and your tendency to romanticize all situations keeps you forever young. Your needs are fueled by all that is gay, humorous, and optimistic; therefore, you take every opportunity to dispel gloom and sadness wherever you encounter it. When depressed or troubled friends look to you for solace, they find it in great and comforting measure. Your popularity is worn well, without conceit, and is richly deserved.

When you allow your negative expression to manifest itself, you fritter away your time, talent, and energy, not to mention funds. Then you idly follow first one thought and then another without appreciating or fulfilling any one of them. You become emotional and flashy in your personal appearance.

Dramatic pursuits, music, and dancing are particularly to your liking, and you should try to get involved in the theater somehow if you are not already so occupied. Speech and all things concerning it—accents, etc.—intrigue you, and you would find yourself interested in one of the opposite sex very quickly if he or she projected a beautiful manner of speech. Your own form of expression is bound to be of a very cultured, intelligent manner, and you will impress others quite easily as a result.

Charm and beauty are as natural to you as the air you breathe. You surround yourself with it, and yet are never aware of it, for it is not at all an affectation. You strive to point out to others how good life can be if they too can see the beauty in everything. You can take pleasure in the fact that you are a marvelous example who does win a good share of converts.

Number 4 Name Expression

You are determined of mind and movement and easily get into the swing of things. Proud and patriotic, you always toe the line and make a good showing of yourself. As steady as the beat of 4/4 time, so is the beat of your reasoning and personal character rhythm.

You are the eternal builder in everything you do, in your profession, social activities, and home life. One by one, every brick of your life will be fitted into place with as much care and consideration as if you were building a house. There is no such thing as your being slipshod and thoughtless in these matters, for it would go against your grain. Therefore, your family will always feel secure and content in the knowledge that you have everything all worked out as accurately and sensibly as is possible.

Honesty and fair play are extremely important to you and you insist on it for all humanity, not just for yourself alone. You are known to family, friends, and employer as the "Rock Of Gibraltar"—you can always be relied upon for good honest opinions and dedicated work.

Far too practical to be a daydreamer, you most likely will not go wandering off around the world in search of romance or adventure, preferring to settle down into a secure, comfortable niche that you carve out for yourself, where you know exactly what to expect and when. No speculation for you.

You know better than anyone that nothing in life is attained without hard work and are conditioned from early on not to expect any more than what you work for. You reap only what you sow, so you concentrate on reality rather than counting on good luck.

Preoccupation with order and organization should not preclude your taking time off to commune quietly with yourself and go over your current endeavors to sort out those that can be weeded out, thus concentrating your strong powers on those that perhaps need more effort.

To rebel against the restricting expression of your number would be unwise, making things extremely uncomfortable and difficult for you. Then nothing will go right, no matter how much effort you expend. Worrying about it will accomplish nothing and will only serve to depress you. You cannot afford the detrimental effects of jealousy and narrow-mindedness, so it would be wise to be grateful for all you have and envy no one.

When you accept the destiny of your Name Expression and live by it, you will be privileged to sit on high and savor the contentment and happiness you have earned.

Number 5 Name Expression

Your inborn love of freedom will never allow you to be forcibly held by anyone or anything. You must always be given plenty of rope to explore as you wish; and when your curiosity is satisfied, you will return willingly and of your own volition. No strings can bind you.

Others often consider you an enigma, and yet your amiability and readiness to adapt to any situation make you a sought-after companion and the life of the party. Your creative imagination is best expressed in words and media that project these ideas, such as writing and all forms of broadcasting.

You have a compulsion to travel the world, see new sights, meet new people, and add to your ever-growing store of knowledge, but you lack the patience required to stay in any one place long enough to become truly adjusted or a part of it, whether it be a city or personal relationship.

The urge to find new interests can be of value if the experience is used in forming new ideas that can be of service to the community or to humanity. Treading the beaten path is not for a restless 5-Expression, but this restlessness will bring about unusual and creative concepts in whatever fields you explore, which will be varied and numerous.

Your adventurous spirit will cause you unhappiness if you allow pressure to weaken your determination to attain your goals. Do not waver in your opinions unless you see a strong possibility that you are wrong. The tendency of a 5 is to run away from opposite opinions and into the face of pleasure.

A strong 5 realizes the danger lurking in such action and will stand up to any adversity, knowing that his or her inventive mind will ferret out a solution eventually. Let the past remain behind you and face each day and its unknown factors with a clear mind and the willingness to meet and conquer the challenge. Possessions, whether material or emotional, can keep you from your higher goals. Travel light through life, clinging to nothing that will hinder you.

The negative 5 lies deplorably and constantly, is ill-tempered, too emotional, and even violent. This person can be ornery, argumentative, and loudmouthed if he or she allows the wastefulness of this negativity to gain control. Patience, tolerance, understanding, and stick-to-it-iveness are all qualities you must cultivate it you are to put the best of your expression to work toward the goals you seek.

Number 6 Name Expression

Responsibility is the key to your complete happiness and success. You thrive on it as a plant does on water; therefore, you are a haven of hope and help for those around you and always manage to find the right logic for any situation. Do not let this take too much out of you, as it no doubt would. Teach the troubled how to handle their own problems and conserve your energies for more important things—you will have many areas in which to expend it.

As a 6-Expression, it's up to you to point out the right direction to family and friends. You are not only the personification of the great protector of hearth and home but a teacher as well.

Truth and justice for all is your motto; the Golden Rule is your code of ethics. No reward is expected for every good deed you do because you realize that to live life to the fullest, doing for others whatever you can is to live in contentment and peace, Therefore, all good things come to you continually from all areas when least expected—and most deservedly so. One of your great joys is establishing a homey atmosphere wherever you may be, which makes for extremely congenial hospitality. As a connoisseur, you enjoy the finer things in life; music, the arts, a beautiful landscape.

Because beauty and harmony are so necessary to your happiness, you go to great lengths to establish both wherever you go, projecting your serenity to everyone with whom you come in contact. This marvelous trait makes you the very best marriage partner.

An excellent conversationalist, you enjoy intellectual discussion, making your true knowledge of affairs a great asset and providing the logic you use to make your point. Never didactic, your word is accepted without question.

Friends always come to you to arbitrate their problems because you are known to be supremely fair and unbiased and will render a just decision. The solutions you suggest usually light the way in a simple but intelligent manner and offer a lifeline to all who need it.

Learn to make quick decisions, knowing that your keen interest in humanity, great intellect, and moral sense will always see you through. Do not under any circumstances allow the negative things in life to influence you. You tend to have emotional highs and lows—times when you are particularly vulnerable. Negativity is your worst enemy—avoid it like the plague! Never forget that you are the great humanitarian of your time, and must never be deterred from your esteemed goals.

Number 7 Name Expression

The total perfectionist, you desire the very best in everything or you will do without all together. Always center stage intellectually, your word and opinion is law. You are not easily induced to attend social affairs, selecting only those you consider worthy. You much prefer your own company, a good book, or the quiet of the country to time spent with uninteresting people. You dislike mingling with a common crowd and are very sensitive to environment, atmosphere, and the personality of those with whom you come in contact.

You are not persuaded easily to make a stand, cautiously keeping your own counsel. However, when approached in the right way, your stored knowledge comes to the fore and you speak authoritatively, particularly where it applies to freedom and peace for all.

Love of variety and constant change is evident in all you do, even in personal relationships, which may include several engagements or marriages. This is a difficult area for you because you cannot stand the thought that you have become dependent on any one person for any reason at all. Then emotional strangulation sets in and the desire for freedom may send you scurrying to check the greener grass on the other side of the fence. The only one able to tie you down will be someone you are unsure of and must strive to hold onto. When you find such a person, you will settle down to this one relationship quite happily, as long as the person keeps you guessing.

Before you find the end of the rainbow you are seeking, you will have many experiences with frequent changes of mind and ideals. This should not deter you as long as you realize that it is necessary to one of your nature to build and grow.

People generally get the impression that they must approach you cautiously, often mistaking your silence for hauteur. This is just a mistaken impression of what is your way of keeping your own counsel. Basically, you have all the traits necessary to become a good friend if someone takes the time to get to know what lies beneath that silent facade: a sensitive and beautiful soul with great depths of sympathy.

All things of an occult nature should be of interest to you because in the true expression of your name lies the sign of the mystic. Study, meditation, and prayer will help you achieve true understanding and the secret of accurately analyzing all things and people. The study of philosophy and metaphysics will help you gain the insight you need.

The strength of your determination to attain your goals will help you weather the many storms that you may encounter along the way. Of a very secretive nature, you can always be trusted to the fullest with any information, and this trait will earn you praise from one and all. Gossiping is not a part of your scheme of things, and you detest it. Keep your head high, undaunted, and the sun will always shine to light the your path.

Because beauty and harmony are so necessary to your happiness, you go to great lengths to establish both wherever you go, projecting your serenity to everyone with whom you come in contact. This marvelous trait makes you the very best marriage partner.

An excellent conversationalist, you enjoy intellectual discussion, making your true knowledge of affairs a great asset and providing the logic you use to make your point. Never didactic, your word is accepted without question.

Friends always come to you to arbitrate their problems because you are known to be supremely fair and unbiased, and will render a just decision. The solutions you suggest usually light the way in a simple but intelligent manner and offer a lifeline to all who need it.

Learn to make quick decisions, knowing that your keen interest in humanity, great intellect, and moral sense will always see you through. Do not under any circumstances allow the negative things in life to influence you. You tend to have highs and lows emotionally, at which times you are particularly vulnerable. Negativity in general is your worst enemy—avoid it like the plague! Never forget that you are the great humanitarian of your time, and must never be deterred from your esteemed goals.

Number 8 Name Expression

Money, power, and success will be the trinity that marks your life pattern, in the true expression of an 8. You have the wonderful quality of transforming ideas into realities. A good memory, well-balanced intellect, and controlled emotions make you a born executive or manager. Keeping everyone happy while busy is a good trait in business. Your usual tact and sense of fair play rub off on others and inspire them to produce on time. Wit and intellect alone, not flattery or emotional outbursts, can impress you and gain your approval.

Diplomacy and courtesy assure a happy and successful marriage—a happier life than if you were single, I might add. A large house that permits gracious entertaining would be the perfect setting for you, allowing you to express the hospitality that is so much a part of your personality. You believe that everyone should share in the wealth and happiness that is available in the world, and this attitude precipitates your involvement in charitable or philanthropic activities. Setting the perfect example, you share all you have with those you love or who are down on their luck. In fact, you may be too giving at times. You are quick to love people who are not in themselves able to give love because you feel they need it and it can bring them a measure of happiness and confidence in themselves. Therefore, you are often terribly hurt.

Endowed with all the power of the almighty 8, you never think small in anything. Your financial deals are apt to be astronomical, and you have no fear of going after whatever you consider worthwhile. Huge sums of money are like a mere pittance to you, though someone with another Name Expression would no doubt be frightened to death. This is an advantage. The responsibilities of high-ranking positions are just your meat and you handle them with confidence and ease. It is only after your financial and emotional goals have been reached that you can enjoy life in the manner you wish. Until that time you will labor on, never losing sight of that pot of gold at the end of the rainbow.

The negative side of your expression can cause great unhappiness if you allow desires for unattained romance, wealth, or power to torment you. Failure, rejection, and discouragement cause you to destroy everything you have achieved, including your peace of mind.

Concentration on your ideals and aspirations, positive thinking, and self-analysis will keep you on the right track to the serenity and high position in life that is your destiny. Wonderful things have been planned for you—accept them with good grace and live up to them. Curb your tendency to allow others to drain you emotionally. Remember, you have the highest of credits in every way, and to be your friend, lover, or mate should be an honor. Don't let anyone topple you off the pedestal you have earned and rightly deserve. Should they attempt to do so, they are not worth your very special brand of unrelenting caring and should be cut out of your life.

Number 9 Name Expression

A 9-Expression is the total of all other numbers; therefore, you have the same qualities with which to develop into a far better person. You can achieve whatever is in your heart because all the powers to command are at your disposal. Goodwill toward others is extremely important to you. Be careful not to be too critical. Your gift of words can get you into trouble.

Set your goal and never swerve from it, no matter what the obstacles might be. See as much of the world as possible, making a point of delving into the soul of everyone you meet, wherever you go. This is necessary to build your understanding of the universe that is yours, according to the expressed destiny of your name.

Love, sympathy, and tolerance highlight your character, precluding the jealousy, envy, or condemnation that hinders the personal progress of some of the other numbers that comprise your total expression. This combination of expressions gives you the built-in power to overcome all the negative traits of this conglomerate

Love is the important key to your happiness—love of humanity and God. This love will surround you to such an extent, filling your life and soul, that unhappiness, loneliness, and earthly upheavals will never affect you. It enables you to face all tests and sacrifices with an additional outpouring of effort and optimism. Disregard the positive aspect of this love or your destined role in life, and you bring upon yourself all the unhappiness, failure, and disappointments the negative 9 projects. There is no need to worry too much on this score, however, because your positive nature is predominant and your life should be one of great happiness and success if you choose to make it so.

The tendency to give too much of yourself or your possessions is strong. Learn to show others how to find the happiness for which they come to you. Conserve your own resources for the time when you need them. Take care of yourself in the best way possible and don't spread your energies too thin. Your service to humanity will bring you everything your heart desires; love, money, success, and good health. You will need all the energy you can manage in order to enjoy them to the fullest.

Fame is far more important to you than material possessions, which really aren't too tempting at all. You would rather be well known for some accomplishment than for your wealth. Words and the media with which to express them are your avenue to this fame. Being in the public eye is food for your soul, and you are at your best before an audience. Cosmopolitan cities of the world are your stage—no country living for you unless it is of a most elegant nature. Luckily, your destiny provides you with the wherewithal to attain and maintain center stage. Accept it, do your best, and enjoy it.

10

Instant Personality Detection

Have you ever wondered, upon meeting someone for the first time, what exactly he or she was like? You don't always have time to get to know someone well enough to assess them accurately, and often that determination is quite important. Numerology is a tool with which you can instantly make an evaluation of anyone and be fairly sure of your first instincts after doing so.

All that is necessary is to commit the first Vowel Indications to memory. The first vowel in the name most commonly used is the one with which you will be concerned. If it is the first letter of the name, it indicates the unadulterated strength of that vowel, but if it is preceded by another letter, it takes on the mitigating vibrations of that letter, thus shading it slightly. However, it is still indicative of the personality involved.

A

You have full confidence in your own ideas and are willing to stand behind them and implement them in whatever way is necessary. You are not at all concerned about what has gone before, precedents or postmortems. If it has not been done before, it is only because no one thought of it, not that it won't work. You ignore caution or criticisms when exploring new ideas or methods and never stop until you are convinced something either will or won't work—that must be your own decision. You always function best when in a position of leadership or when you can express your ideas. You don't mind being the first to undertake any venture and really don't care if you have to do so alone, for the faith you have in yourself always sustains you. Always striving, always searching, always first in your Golden Rule for yourself.

E

A change of pace, change of people, and change of ideas is the keynote to those with this first vowel indicator. Variety is the spice of their life and constant pursuit of such variety is their greatest pleasure. All of this makes them interesting and exciting individuals, and extremely popular, since they can add something to relationships that few others can. They can express themselves in a vivid, colorful manner that makes others live vicariously through them, and thus inject some excitement into their own lives. Ever on the move, if not physically, certainly mentally, they develop a quick interest and grasp of the facts in almost any subject brought to their attention. They are invariably attractive and popular with the opposite sex. Their wide experience, coupled with innate wisdom and perception, make them excellent judges of character; and they can usually see two sides of another's personality equally, always accepting the good with the bad. This makes them excellent mates or friends.

I

This vowel gives individuals the capability of running the gamut of emotions and experiences. They want almost everything in life and cannot see why they cannot have it all immediately. They won't settle for the mundane and always shoot for the stars. Travel, the arts, fame, and fortune are the four cornerstones of their ambition, and chances are they will attain these things somehow or other. They have it within their hearts to show every kind of emotion, even though there are times when it is detrimental to themselves. A soft touch by all means, they can always be relied upon to lend a soft shoulder or financial assistance, whatever the need may be, even if it is their last cent. Love is a desperate need for such a person and they give wholly of themselves in this way. To be loved by someone with such vibrations is to know the truest form of this emotion, and they attract it in like manner.

O

Responsibility personified, you have here a person of great strength who is capable of the kind of sympathy, understanding, and tolerance that makes the world go round.

They can always be counted on for a true statement of problems and a workable solution to overcome them, even when the rest of us are blind to them. Beauty surrounds them and they give off a quiet serenity that cannot help but affect those with whom they are connected. A true friend, wise mediator, and loving mate; this is a person worth knowing. They are munificently generous and enjoy spreading happiness wherever they go. Tact and diplomacy distinguish them, and intelligence and charm are significant assets.

U

Sparkle and gaiety are the two words that best describe those with this vowel as their indicator. They are full of *joie de vivre* and the life of every party. People are easily drawn to them and their friends are legion. To be a friend or mate of such a person is indeed a pleasure, for they cannot help but imbue you with the same spirit of gaiety by which they live. In business they are a great asset because customers or clients always respond favorably to them. A lover of beauty in all forms, they can make even a gray cloud appear colorful, and seek to see only the bright side of life. Depression is unknown to them and, therefore, they can always be counted on to lift one's spirits. A whole new understanding of life is yours if you attach yourself to such a person. A pure esthete, all things respond to him or her, because they will it so.

Y

Introspective and perceptive souls lie under the quiet exteriors of these individuals. They think twice about absolutely everything and never make hasty judgments. When they have made up their minds, their decision is final, inasmuch as much deliberation goes into that decision They are good judges of character and very particular about those they choose to accept in their inner circle of trust and friendship. They are almost impossible to get to know, but once you break down the barrier, you will find them worth the trouble; their intelligence and perception can open many new areas of interest or study for you. Their opinions should be taken into consideration in all situations since these are generally quite valid and unemotionally arrived at. They have no regard for tawdry or uncouth behavior.

OW

This person must be given his or her head and you must not try to suppress their intuitive qualities, for they are blessed with a master power that must be utilized to the fullest. To suppress them is to reduce them to nothing, which would be a crime. They can point the way where others see only darkness and they can be trusted to lead only in the right direction, for seldom do they lose their way. They are of a very cooperative nature if they see that you care about them. They need love and prefer to work in conjunction with others, especially of the opposite sex. They must be their own boss and have to be free to function as such, if not in business then surely in their private lives. They have to be respected and it is never misplaced. They are possessed of a compelling personality that reminds one of the Pied Piper, in that we follow them willingly and are always richer for having done so. Enlightenment is their aim—one they generally achieve.

OY

Here we see a complex of detail and concentration. This person can boil down massive facts and distill them into the very basics, so necessary to the foundation of a project. He or she can take these facts and start constructing what no one else was able to perceive, but stay out of their way and do not try to derail them or take up any of their precious time on frivolity, for they have a devotion to the task that few others can claim. They rarely stop until the job is completed to the tiniest detail; and only when the last touch has been applied, will they step back and observe. Until then they cannot let their attention waiver and resent any intrusion. Do not disagree with them or try to question their purpose or methods unless you are prepared for a most enervating confrontation. Be armed with unalterable facts.

EW

You have the double 5-Vibrancy that endows you with great sales ability, and you should be able to sell anything you have a mind to, be it product or idea. The field of rejuvenation methods would be particularly successful for you. You must be careful in the emotional department because you are quite vulnerable here. It is a necessity for you to be involved always with a member of the opposite sex, either in business or in a personal way, for you function better then, but you do have to learn to understand them better and, until you do, there will no doubt be painful experiences. Keep in mind that each one is another brick in the foundation of life and eventually you will benefit from them. Eventually, too, you will emerge as a very intuitive, understanding individual, appreciated by all.

11

Missing Links

We often hear the phrase that someone is "missing a few marbles," and I'm afraid that it's quite a true statement. The truth of the matter is that almost every human being is missing a few marbles, except that in reality they are missing a few links.

We say of people that they lack understanding, patience, tolerance, ambition, etc. We also hear as an excuse for marital incompatibility that "you never really know a person until you live with him or her." On this understatement, many marriages do in fact flounder. Where there are children involved, the disagreements can so warp the family that the children in turn develop complexes of their own.

When a woman contemplates marriage, she may consider a man's background, position, and future prospects very carefully; and yet it is the inherent personality and well-hidden basic characteristics that really bear looking into and are too well camouflaged to be seen.

Women are often accused of being devious and, let's face it, gals, we are. When we are with that special someone, we put our best foot forward, smile when we feel like frowning, laugh when we want to scream, and pretend to accept when we really reject his ideas or attitudes—all because we want him. Subconsciously, we harbor the thought that we will change him after he is hooked. If you haven't already made this blunder—don't! The only way a man really changes is when he and he alone decides he wants to. Spare yourself the agony of finding out the hard way where the obstacles lie by checking the Missing Links in his name that can tell you what is lacking in him. And of course, all this advice goes for men as well, to check out the women in their lives.

The missing letters in a name will act as your own special undercover agent. Print the name in full and below each letter its corresponding number, following the chart below. Then make three rows of numbers as per the example in chapter 9. Put a check next to each number for every time the number appears in the name.

NUMBERS & CORRESPONDING LETTERS								
1	2	3	4	5	6	7	8	9
A	B	C	D	E	F	G	H	I
J	K	L	M	N	O	P	Q	R
S	T	U	V	W	X	Y	Z	

Example: J O H N   S M I T H
         1 6 8 5   1 4 9 2 8

1) 2   4) 1   7) 0
2) 1   5) 1   8) 2
3) 0   6) 1   9) 1

In the above example we see a lack of any 3s or 7s. To find out what characteristics are missing as a result, check the following descriptions.

Keep in mind that these Missing Links only indicate areas where improvement is needed if the individual is aware of such a lack. Even the most distasteful of traits can be reversed if this guide is used and the desire to do so exists.

The total combination is also to be considered, so it is possible that other powers inherent in the individual help to make up for the lack. Since each name carries a different vibratory combination of numbers, it is impossible to make blanket statements here for all. Each name must be considered in conjunction with its Destiny Number as well. The descriptions given here merely indicate the traits that are most likely to be lacking in regard to the number they are represented by, in a singular sense, not in it's total concept. (The number/letter correspondences chart is repeated on page 174 for your convenience.)

Number 1 Vibration

The lack of this vibration can be a severe hardship, if the power of leadership or creativity is necessary to attain the kind of success desired. You can, of course, achieve this goal through inheritance or marriage, and certainly through application of your own talents. You will also find it more difficult to overcome destructive pitfalls in your life easily. There can be no ego problem because those without a 1-Vibration do not have an overly developed 1. That in some cases can be problematical because everyone needs an ego of sorts. To be devoid of it is to be devoid of self-love or the desire to get ahead.

Much opposition generally dances in attendance on one lacking this vibration and he or she will have to strive very hard to withstand the criticism and make his own way. The objections will cause friction that they may be unable to obviate.

There will no doubt be much "leading-by-the-nose" in the life of one with this lack and, for someone in a top position, this can be tragic.

This person will most likely be heckled and ignored in relationships because he or she will not have the ability to stand up to their mate.

In every relationship, generally one of the parties has a strong personality, so for the other this lack of the 1-Vibration can be a blessing as it will lead to little friction. It's helpful for one half of the couple to do the leading, and the other not to fear the lack of domineering leadership in their own personality. It will be easier to accept the wishes and orders of someone else if one does not have to fight to suppress their own need for superiority. There will be no need to wish to debate the position of leadership if one partner has no desire for it, so there would be no clash of tempers in this regard. For people lacking these powers, however, it would be well to take a more definite stand on the things that really involve them and develop more willpower and creativity.

Number 2 Vibration

Since 2 is the number of cooperation, you will have to expect little patience or assistance from one without its powers. To be missing such a trait means that you will be a strong, overpowering individual with little understanding or desire to be cooperative. It would be well to find a 2 in the name of either a partner or mate in order to be assured of loyalty and the kind of cooperation that is necessary in such relationships. You can rely on a person without this number to be detached in a sense and to have little regard for the feelings of others, while demanding perfect understanding and sympathy for him- or herself.

The head of a family or business can more easily get along without this power, but it is necessary to cultivate the art of giving in and consideration if he or she is involved with others in a business sense. True, other traits can make up for it. If the other powers are there, this person may have such innate intelligence that cooperation is not as important to him. It will be more important to create and build and leave the cooperation to others. Nevertheless, everyone should have some small amount of it in order to make the best of things.

Someone without this number will have to try to develop more patience and concern for others. They must not rush things and be in a hurry for everything. This can lead to shabby results that they will be unhappy with in the long run. Diplomacy is another trait that must be developed.

Number 3 Vibration

There will be a decided lack of artistic talents here and a tendency to perhaps live vicariously through the talents of others as a result. You may hold yourself in instead of allowing yourself to express all that you feel, for fear of being rejected on the grounds of being a "know nothing." This may lead you to strive for attention in other ways, which may not be too satisfactory. Garish clothes or manners can never give you the right kind of attention or satisfaction you seek in true, lasting relationships.

Nothing is beyond comprehension if you put your mind to it, and the same applies to talent or some special field of endeavor. You can acquire good skills and command respect and admiration if you take the time and trouble to do so and can then be on the same level of acceptance as those you admire.

It is necessary to spend as much time as possible with diversified groups of people and try to absorb every word and scrap of knowledge possible.

Cultivate especially those who do have talent, preferably in the artistic sense. Literature is a worthy study if you lack the vibrations of a 3. You should try to cultivate an interest in books and use the knowledge gained so you will feel completely at home and can discuss them with knowledgeable people.

Concentrate on self-expression and perfection of your manner of speech. Do not lower yourself to idle chitchat of a catty or harmful nature. It can do you no good at all, when the same conversation can be an enlightening one instead, from which either you or your companions can learn something of value.

Lack of the 3 influence could cause one to dwell on the shallow, meaningless things in life, and this should be avoided at all costs. Though it may take a great deal of effort initially to avoid such a situation, concentration on higher goals will eventually turn the tide and create an aura of activity and success around you.

Number 4 Vibration

Lack of this vibration can definitely cause a bit of a problem because there can be little concentration on work or all the details involved in successfully completing the chores that are necessary to everyday living, whether it be in business or the home. It indicates a tendency toward being slipshod, a trait that must certainly be overcome with all due haste, for nothing can ever come of it. The 4-Vibration gives strength and determination—to be without it lessens that strength.

Personalities lacking in this vibration are lax in all ways. They continually run away from responsibilities, problems, and all matters requiring thought or effort. When things get out of hand as a result of their neglect, they get upset and try to run away from them rather than face them head-on and take care of them. They are always in a state of confusion, and their emotions fluctuate greatly. They have continual periods of alternating highs and lows, with few periods of calm, smooth sailing in between. Life is always chaotic for such people and therefore it is harder for them to achieve any great happiness or contentment. Success, too, usually eludes them as they do not have the stamina or concentration necessary to attain this success. At the same time, they resent this lack of success and become depressed at what they feel is a run of bad luck.

This type of person must most definitely condition him- or herself to the fact that everything in life can be had if they just put in the necessary thought and labor, and then strive to stick with a job from its inception to its conclusion. Once a measure of satisfaction or success is attained from such application of efforts, it will be easier to understand the necessity for it. This person will find it easier to fall into this new routine, thus eventually gaining all that is wished for. This applies to personal relationships as well as business activities. Health must be watched, because it, too, can suffer from lack of care or attention until it is too late. In short, avoid laziness or irresponsibility of any kind.

Number 5 Vibration

Here is a personality that takes quite a bit of understanding and cultivation; it is one of hesitation and seclusion—if not in the real sense of social involvement, then surely in an intellectual and spiritual sense. You will find that someone lacking this vibration can be terribly introverted and afraid to face the normal adversities of life or social intercourse.

Not only do such people reject the normal involvement of life but they also reject others who prefer to involve themselves actively in any manner or endeavor on both the business and social levels. They shrink from this kind of activity and, as a result, are terribly unsympathetic to humanity in general. They tend to wrap themselves in a cloak of unfeeling, unseeing negativity. They cannot step out freely or enthusiastically to taste life in all its glory. That enjoyment and excitement can be theirs for the taking may be incomprehensible and repulsive to them.

These people are afraid to try anything new, whether it be in relationships, emotions, business, or just plain living. They set a dull unrelenting pattern for themselves and seldom waiver from this throughout their whole life.

They would do well to develop an interest in all things around us and a true feeling for humanity. They should step out into the sunlight of life, and open their minds and hearts to all that is there to experience, to run the gamut of emotions and learn the joy of loving and the knowledge that comes from pain. It's important to broaden their scope and knowledge to the point of being able to understand other people and all their foibles.

Only then can you grow as a person and gain the necessary stature and success that could be such joy. Meet every situation head-on, knowing that from it will come the sort of experience that will prepare you for future problems. Open your eyes, mind, and heart, and life will be full and exciting.

Number 6 Vibration

This can be a difficult person to live with, in more ways than one. The understanding, tolerance, and sympathy so necessary in daily living and association with others is missing here, unless other numbers compensate for it.

One devoid of a 6-Vibration can be a bit too fond of self with no desire to understand that others have personalities and problems of their own that need consideration. It must be learned that everyone is entitled to his or her own personal point of view even if it happens to be different from yours. Responsibility will be great in life, and a tendency to shirk those responsibilities is inherent in one with no 6-Vibration to shore them up when they need the strength to shoulder problems. It could mean that one is confined, and this could go against the grain, unless the necessity is understood. It may mean that you cannot finish the things you have already started or wish to start and that can rankle a weak person easily. Fours in a name can mitigate this weakness, of course.

Since a "Missing Link" only refers to a tendency, which means that it is not an insurmountable problem, all missing traits can be developed. The 2s, 3s, and 5s make the lack of a 6-Vibration barely noticeable.

So there is hope here. Concentrate on getting to know and understand all those with whom you are in contact. You are bound to experience some very unhappy and unsettling situations in your life, and, as you gain the acceptance and understanding of each one of them, you will grow as a person until you can bounce back easily and turn every adversity into an asset.

Love of others is very important in life and can only be enjoyed if it is freely given. You need this and can revel in it when you inspire others to give it of their own volition. Do not try to change those you care about, making them conform to your idea of what they should be.

Number 7 Vibration

Most likely, one without the vibratory power of the 7 has an "I'm from Missouri, show me" attitude. They are not too easily convinced if they have made up their minds to some contrary opinion, particularly insofar as an understanding of philosophy, psychology, or other such subjects is concerned. They would be very skeptical and even annoyingly averse to discussions of these subjects, having a closed mind and being unwilling to even listen to such a discussion, no matter what facts or opinions are presented.

On the other hand, they may go completely overboard and become rather eccentric with no even balance. Neither attitude is advantageous, and one must attempt to maintain a sensible outlook that can either accept or reject a theory based only on facts available. Emotionally, the lack of a 7-Vibration tends to make them terribly introverted and unable to express any emotion, no matter how much they desire to do so. They just don't seem to know how to go about it and suffer greatly because they themselves require the kind of soul-satisfying emotional relationships that make the world go round. They don't trust others or themselves in such matters and therefore hold themselves aloof from these situations. Needless to say, this is a very unhealthy situation and must eventually erupt in some sort of corrosion emotionally. The tendency then is to relieve the spirit in demeaning ways such as misusing alcohol, drugs, and other forms of degradation that only compound the agonies already suffered.

It is necessary here to let down the barriers and try to express what is felt without reservation. Say what you think and delve into what is unknown to you. Take every opportunity to experience, learn, and express all phases of your emotions. Be interested in others and allow them to reach out to you.

Number 8 Vibration

Since the number 8 reflects material gain in this world, this is where anyone lacking this number will feel the pinch. They will always seem to be just outside the realm of attaining the material possessions or wealth they desire—at least in such a way that it comes easily. Naturally, it can be earned through hard work or it can be inherited. But we know that it is not destined irrevocably from the vibration of the name.

Because of this it would be a constant worry and it would be well to cultivate the habit of living within your means and counting only on what you yourself can acquire through your daily efforts. In other words, no pie-in-the-sky dreaming. Resist the temptation to rob Peter to pay Paul and get in over your head financially.

It may be difficult to accept the fact that great wealth is not yours for the asking, but once you do, you will be happier and more resigned to reality. This will open the door to a more normal set of circumstances, and you can acquire much that you desire by setting your sights realistically and working toward them.

You may find yourself worrying needlessly over bills because of your highly developed sense of monetary values and therefore you should take care to live well within your means and obviate any necessity for concern. The tendency to judge everything according to its monetary worth can distort your true appraisal of things. Stop thinking in dollar signs and you will discover the basic happiness in life that is yours for the taking, with no price tag attached. When money does come your way, use it wisely, with an eye toward the future and practicality. Don't give in to your innermost urge to splurge recklessly.

Number 9 Vibration

Without the sympathetic and understanding vibrations of the 9, individuals may be a bit too unconcerned about their fellow humans and can give the impression of being extremely hard-shelled. It would be hard to tolerate what does not agree with your own opinion and very difficult to relent when you have made up your mind to do something a certain way.

Appealing to your better nature is of no value because it cannot be swayed by emotions. You prefer to remain aloof from the problems of those with whom you are concerned because you do not wish to become entangled in anyone else's affairs, especially if there is trouble. However, you will have to learn that only when you do become involved with people, in their unhappy as well as happy situations, can you begin to reap the rewards of true love and friendship. Until then you will never know what it is to really belong to anyone. A 6 in your name can help here, however.

You are bound to be disappointed in an *affaire d'amour* because it will necessitate deep emotion and trust, which you do not come by easily. You must learn to let down your hair and accept people on faith, then give of yourself freely. The more you give, the more you find will be returned.

If you keep an open mind and heart, you will slowly see the happiness that can be yours by so giving.

Take a deep interest in people, their problems, and what is going on around you in the world. Broaden your outlook and concentrate less on what you want out of life. The less you worry about being hurt the less vulnerable you will become.

Try to anticipate the need of help by your family and friends, and offer whatever assistance you can without being asked and without thought of reward, whether it be material or spiritual in nature. In short, develop sympathy, understanding, and love for all the world.

12

Personal Harmony by Destiny Number

In any relationship, be it friendship, business, romance, or marriage, there is a certain amount of give-and-take, or maneuvering if you will, that is necessary to assure success. It is not always so easy to know exactly what someone else thinks or feels deep down inside, and that is what makes it so difficult to always do or say just the right thing to keep a relationship on an even keel.

You may have romantic visions about someone with whom you would be better off in business than in romance. Or perhaps you are interested in someone with whom you are constantly at odds. Do you love your mate desperately, but can't seem to get along with him or her?

By using the Personal Harmony Vibration, you can tell at a glance what your compatibility with any individual is and how best to handle the situation for satisfactory results.

This is an ideal way to plot the course of a romance or to assure clear sailing in a marriage, friendship, or business relationship.

To determine the compatibility of yourself and another person, you must first determine your Destiny Numbers. Add together the number of the month, day, and year of birth and reduce to a single digit. Example: the birth dates of June 6, 1965, and June 29, 1971, would be calculated as follows:

6 (for June) +6+1+9+6+5=27=9
6 (for June) +2+9+1+9+7+1=35=8

To find the compatibility of these two numbers, look for the 9-Personal Harmony by Destiny Number (page 209) and then for the 8-Compatibility reading that follows it (page 211). Keep in mind that the vibrations of the name and other factors also enter into it, so this is just one form of illuminating someone's character. Take all prospects into consideration.

Destiny Number 1

Compatibility with Destiny Number:

1 A good combination in just about every way. You are both intelligent and perceptive. There isn't much you two cannot accomplish together if you put your minds to it. Recognize the fact that the other party has the same incentives you do and do not try to take the lead all the time. Instead, cooperate equally for total success in everything.

2 Every combination needs one leader and one cooperative partner. Such is the case here. You are the leader and the other party ably assists you, showing indomitable powers of cooperation and ability to handle all the details. This works well for any sort of relationship: business, marriage, or friendship.

3 The other party has all the personality and charm necessary to interest others in your projects, or to attract to you a warm circle of friends. You, on the other hand, have the ideas and initiative to lead this duo to great success. There is no conflict of purpose or personality here, so you should work well together and go far in whatever you do.

4 Whatever plans or ideas you initiate will be worked out to the finest detail by the other party, who has all the powers of concentration and hard work, while you provide the leadership and incentive. This is a good blending of brains and brawn, though it doesn't necessarily mean physical labor. You may change course often, but the other party will steer you back onto the path of project completion, so give them equal consideration.

5 The 5-Vibration calls for self-expression in the form of words, plus an element of change, travel, and excitement. If you remember this and do not try to suppress the expression of the other party, all should be well. Your inventiveness can direct the efforts and enthusiasm of others as long as it is creative or suggestive, rather than dictatorial.

6 The 6-Personality is one who loves home, people, and culture. They prefer to be led with love and intelligence, not by a dictatorial manner. Insisting on doing things your way is not the way to get along with this type of person. Be gentle, phrase your ideas in the form of suggestions, and you should get along very well. Get involved in the arts.

7 You are inventive and oriented toward leadership, while the other party is a deep thinker. Blend these talents carefully and you should prosper financially. A 7 cannot be ordered about and resents heavy demands, so you will have to sublimate your forceful ideas or manner. Intellectually, you will get on very well if you interest yourself in philosophy.

8 A good combination if you stick to your goals. You can lead this duo to great happiness with your basic intelligence, and the other party can add a strong vibration of fame and power which you will both profit from. Take your time and be sure that your aims are worthy, to avoid friction. Honesty and justice are very important here. Discuss all ideas thoroughly and give serious thought to everything projected by your partner.

9 Again, you take the lead, while you can count on the other party for support, understanding, and sympathy when needed. Whatever you decide to do will generally be of interest to the other, but if not, do not allow yourself to be swayed. Your creativity should excite your partner if you exhibit it in an interesting way, as their curiosity is strong. A 9-Vibration is ever curious and will go along with you on just about anything.

Destiny Number 2

Compatibility with Destiny Number:

1 With the other party contributing the ideas and inventiveness, you can be very happy carrying out the execution of those plans. As marital partners, yours is the role of acquiescence, while the other will take the reins and make the decisions. You really won't mind this though and actually prefer it that way. Your partner will appreciate your patience and cooperation, and your bond will be strong.

2 There will be no argument about duties or leadership here, for as 2s you will share equally the burdens, responsibilities, or successes of your union. As marital partners, you would have an ideal marriage. If not overly wealthy, you will possess the kind of happiness that only comes from sharing, with no competition as to who knows best. Peace reigns supreme in such a relationship—a nice, steady, and calm duo.

3 Confine your efforts in this combination to that of winning friends and charming people. The other party will be better able to direct the involvement of your association, and you can rely on their decisions to be in your best interests. Keep calm and accept whatever comes your way without animosity or disagreement. Control your temper and jealousy.

4 A good workable team is this combination. The other party is the supreme builder, and a good foundation will be laid in any and all of the projects you undertake together. Your offering will be in the assistance and encouragement you give, for you are the most cooperative of numbers. You will fare well in marriage, business, or friendship.

5 Your partner in this duo will be the center of the stage and lend charm, vivacity, creativity, and excitement to your combination. You, on the other hand will bask in the glory and enjoy it, since you don't really care to take the spotlight in any case. However, you have more of a sense of stability and you should use it whenever necessary.

6 Materially, you two will find great success, as marriage or business are equally well favored. The other person should always hold the reins, while you execute the plans. They will generally be right when it comes to making decisions as their second sense assures this. However, your cooperation is the catalyst for success.

7 Where work in any of the psychic fields is involved, you will find a good blending of the minds here. However, you will be called upon often to lend moral support or to endure long silences, as 7s are given to moodiness at times. A 2 is well equipped to

handle this tactfully and gracefully, with the understanding that is needed, so all will be well.

8 Financially, this is a good team and should always
have the best of everything. The 8 brings the power
of financial advances, while you lend your assistance
and cleverness. You have the reputation of being
straight and honest, adding to the good vibrations
that the two of you can use to your betterment. Aid
and assist in every way possible.

9 A good duo indeed in that you each add to the
other's personality and interest. You can bolster
each other whenever the need arises. Your partner is
creative and imaginative, while you are practical and
efficient. Follow your hearts desire as you feel the
need, and chances are you can interest the other
party if you appeal to his imagination.

Destiny Number 3

Compatibility with Destiny Number:

1 Your charm and vivacity, coupled with the intelligence and leadership of your partner, makes this a
very powerful combination. You can accomplish
anything you wish, for you will fire each other with
the excitement and practical application of new ideas.
You will both enjoy good living and popularity, but
don't spread yourselves too thin. Stay focused.

2 Where you are vivacious and outgoing, your partner
is stable and practical, which is what you need to

keep you from dissipating your talents and energies. In business the part of the "front man" should be taken by you, while your partner keeps things flowing smoothly behind the scenes. In a personal relationship, you can keep a pleasant balance.

3 You should be quickly drawn to any other 3-Vibration, for you are identical in attitude and personality. You will always know exactly what the other will think and do. If you use this knowledge wisely, there should be no friction. You would do well in projects that deal with education, should you be involved in an impersonal way. Marriage is also well favored, and this is an extremely passionate and sexual combustion as well.

4 You may not react too favorably to the down-to-earth attitude of the other party, for the vibration there is for a no-nonsense one. You, on the other hand, prefer a more loosely knit arrangement. It would be to your benefit if you could accept the stabilizing influence this party could have on you. They will give you a better sense of peace and tranquility.

5 The other party has a great capacity for new ideas and excitement and is apt to delve into them more quickly than you might on your own. Your relationship will be constantly on the move. The other party will always want to get right on with it without hesitation—therefore, you will feel more active, which will eventually build your own strength and determination. You will become more adventurous and curious as a result.

6 This should be a happy relationship, with your vivaciousness plus the other party's sense of proportion. Where you may tend to be a bit too frivolous or irresponsible at times, they will lend support and common sense, making for an even balance. Pay heed and be grateful. Your mind and world will expand for your mutual benefit.

7 This could be a profitable combination, for there is a great deal of creativity inherent in this combination. Your talents and ideas should blend extremely well and there should be little difficulty in getting along on a creative basis. You will take turns in arousing the interest of the other, and this will trigger new projects of great benefit to the two of you.

8 If you listen to this person and do not insist on holding the reins, this could be one of the happiest relationships of your lifetime. All you ever hoped for can be found within this combination. You may have the charm and personality, but the other person has the intelligence and financial know-how that will lead to success in almost everything. An 8-Vibration generally brings fame, power, and fortune. Lucky you.

9 Here it is important for you to be a good listener and to learn at the feet of your partner. They have the wisdom and common sense, plus logic, that can

lead to satisfactory results in any undertaking if you let them take the lead. They are also very intuitive, where you are more inclined to frivolity, so heed their advice and react without hesitation.

Destiny Number 4

Compatibility with Destiny Number:

1 As long as you are content to let the other person make all the decisions and create the ideas and methods by which you will abide, all will be well. You will be the one to stick to business, or the marital partner with the practical and determined mind who can best follow through on your mate's initiative. Do not allow resentment of their leadership to occur or to color your judgment, because it really is to your benefit.

2 There should no problem here at all. You complement each other perfectly in that you both respect the other's talents and ideas, and there is no question of jostling for a position of leadership between you. There should be understanding, respect, and true friendship or love between you, depending upon your relationship. This is a good marital combination.

3 Great possibilities here if you take the role of second-in-command. The other party will be the stronger candidate for leader in all your endeavors, whereas your unique powers of practicality and perseverance make you the perfect assistant or mate in this case. However, you must try to be tolerant, sympathetic, and patient. You won't regret it.

4 What a strong duo you two are. There is little that you cannot accomplish together. There is a strong vibration for all the success, money, and happiness that you desire, since you will both work hard at it. Luckily, the combined forces here bode well for humanity, and you should use your assets to further the understanding, health, and happiness of people throughout the world. You will then also experience great joy and a sense of great accomplishment.

5 You will have to be the strong member of this combination for the other person tends to be a bit more flighty or fickle. He or she may wish to change horses in midstream, but you will have to keep things at an even pace. Pay attention to these wants, but follow your own impulses too as they will no doubt be the leveling factor needed for both of you.

6 This should be a very profitable and pleasurable relationship if you work together on all things. Give each other full cooperation and consideration and you will reap great rewards. There is a good vibration here for creativity and intelligent use of your talents and efforts. You should devise original techniques or ideas together for monetary gain.

7 This person has strong powers of meditation and concentration that will give birth to a wealth of ideas and methods that can be extremely profitable to you both. Your role will be that of the practical executioner of these ideas. Where the other person is mental in her or his pursuit of happiness and success, you are physical, which is a good, balanced combination, and neither of you will step on the other's toes.

8 A great deal of gaiety is inherent here and you should have a very pleasant relationship, always full of fun and games. It promises to produce financial success in in business affairs. As a combination for marriage, it is also a good one. Always show whatever sympathy and understanding is needed by the other party; it will be greatly appreciated and contribute to the solidarity of your union.

9 Your practical nature will see this relationship through to successful conclusions in all your dealings. The other person has the inventiveness and intelligence to provide the fuel for this machine, so pay heed to the thoughts and ideas expressed. You, too, have a flair for inventiveness at times, so don't hesitate to add your own two cents' worth.

Destiny Number 5

Compatibility with Destiny Number:

1 Give the other person their fair share of the limelight and try to pay heed to their ideas, for they will be good ones. You have the vivacious spirit and constant drive for new methods or fields to explore, while the other person has great powers of creativity.

This makes for an exciting duo. You both have great
stores of energy and curiosity. Use them.

2 This could be one of those relationships that can go
either way. The other person is not strong enough to
take the lead and you have the desire to do so, but
you could tire of their passiveness if you do not
recognize the finer qualities this person possesses.
Guide your relationship lovingly if it is one of
romance, and carefully if one of business.

3 No problems here at all. You complement each
other perfectly and should accomplish all you wish.
Success is inherent, and you can attain all you ever
wanted by treating each other with understanding
and respect. Since you have strong vibrations of
charity here, you will do exceptionally well in any
kind of charity or organizational capacity together.

4 In you the other person finds the antithesis of
him- or herself and will bask in all you represent,
so beware of taking unfair advantage of that
admiration. Treat them with kindness and understanding, as well as complete fairness and honesty.
Your mate may be too cautious and practical, but
you can lead him or her gently to a more expedient
way of doing things.

5 You really have to work at this one, and it will not be
easy. Tempers will have to be kept in constant check
for you are both given to quick exasperation with
people. Since you are both beset with wanderlust,

you will have to take into consideration that there comes a time when one must settle down. There will be many breakups and reconciliations in this duo—all of a very passionate nature.

6 Though the other person is kind, humane, and intelligent, your vivaciousness and curiosity lend the luster to this relationship, and the two of you act as a good balance for each other. Your partner has a well-honed intelligence that can benefit both of you if you take the time to bring it out. Allow the other person the opportunity to shine, and listen well. They are very peace and family oriented, which makes for a good foundation in a relationship.

7 The other half of this duo may prove to be a bit of a trial to you, as he or she is not apt to look kindly upon your constant inquisitiveness and continual conversation, but is more meditative and prefers the quiet, spiritual type of silences necessary to form opinions or concepts, rather then incessant prattling. Learn to recognize and honor these periods.

8 Here you must learn to listen and defer to the other person's wisdom whenever important decisions are to be made. They have a more steady, practical nature than you do, and you can gain much by trying to cooperate with them. He or she will generally select the best road for you to travel and thereby open new vistas that you may not otherwise have known.

9 This is a bright, productive relationship where both parties lend equal support and enthusiasm. You will be well balanced because you inspire and bring out the best in each other. You are vivacious and active, which the other person appreciates, while he or she is steadier and inventive enough to stimulate you. Where you are humorous your mate is adventurous, foresighted, and intuitive—a good combination.

Destiny Number 6

Compatibility with Destiny Number:

1 You have the charitable and practical nature that is a good foundation for the other person's original and creative attitude. You can be of great assistance to the other, but it is best for them to take the lead. You can always lend support and the wisdom that comes from your great love of humanity. This is a good combination for charitable works.

2 Financially, you should do well together because the combined vibration is one of material supply. Your intellect will spawn the ideas or methods by which you can attain this wealth, while the other person's fine powers of cooperation and assistance will see that they are implemented properly to bring about this success. Organizational works are also well favored, and you will get rewards back in spades.

3 This will be a relationship of long duration, so you will want to put all your best efforts into it. You get on well together as you have many of the same traits and understand each other perfectly. The other person has a stronger personality and expresses exactly what he feels at all times, where you tend toward a more quiet nature, but you will be happy together, whether in business or marriage, and never bored.

4 You will always want to make sure that there are no temper tantrums here or you will lose all the powers that can be of mutual benefit. You are both hard-working types and can gain much from your association. It is doubtful that many problems will exist between you, leaving you free to function well in the creative areas you both enjoy.

5 This could be a very important relationship and one that should not be treated lightly. The other person is highly intellectual and creative and can add much to this duo if you pay strict attention to what they have to say and do. You can learn much from them. You, on the other hand, have many exciting experiences and versatility to lend to the duo.

6 A peaceful and relaxing relationship is indicated here in that you are both the same type of people. You like all the same things and your minds run along the same avenues. You bring out the best in each other and blend into one harmonious combination—a bit serious perhaps, but you make the most of your time, and the projects upon which you embark are very worthwhile, so do whatever appeals to you and do it with pleasure.

7 This is not what could be called a perfect blend, as you are of completely opposite minds and natures. The other person may be a bit too contemplative for your easygoing nature, and it could be irritating. A great amount of compromising is called for if you are to make this combination work. You will have to start with the little things and cautiously build on them, but don't expect it to be an easy or blissful ride.

8 In this relationship, you will find a greater measure of success and happiness if you let the other person take the lead and you play the role of stabilizer. There is a possibility of lots of "blue sky" talk and plans; you will have to sort out the worthwhile projects and concentrate on them. Do not be misled by flowery conversation. Logic prevails.

9 A very good, solid relationship is indicated here— one that bears pursuing. You have everything in common and understand each other and your mutual goals perfectly. This is the rare sort of combination that can fare well in any sort of situation; business, friendship, or marriage. You enhance each other's basic qualities and trigger the best in each other.

Destiny Number 7

Compatibility with Destiny Number:

1 If material possessions are your goal, this is a fortuitous combination and all things should come to you together. The other person will be in a better position to take the helm, and you will function well in the capacity of thinker. You have the ability to delve deeply and see the pitfalls or potential of the project while the other person is overenthusiastic.

2 This will be a quiet and peaceful relationship as you are both cooperative and reserved by nature. When the other person wishes to be alone with you, you will be more than happy to oblige, since the bright social lights hold no fascination for either of you. The study of the occult, metaphysics, or philosophy could be of great delight to both of you, as you are both so inclined. This is a very comfortable duo, with peaceful prospects.

3 The other person in this combination will be the gay, flitting, charming partner, while you sit back and enjoy all the activity, for you are the more quiet of the two. At times it may appear to be a bit much, but you will have to contain yourself and try to understand if you want to get on well together. You can use a bit of livening-up in any case.

4 This is a powerful combination if you put your mind to it. In anything creative, you have a strong chance of success. Your agile and contemplative mind can create the ideas and methods that the other party will implement beautifully. A good blending of the physical and mental typifies such a combination. There should be no friction in this strong union.

5 You will need a lot of patience because this duo could be a bit of a trial unless you keep your head at all times. This other person is quite flighty, by your standards, and there will be times of friction and great disagreement, particularly due to their constantly changing mind. You are a stable individual and find it difficult to understand the wanderings of the other. If you manage to overlook it you can get on well, but it will take tenacity.

6 This may be a very difficult relationship for you to reconcile yourself to as you are more reclusive and withdrawn and the other party is more outgoing, which you will not always appreciate. If you are determined to try, you will have to find great inner strength to draw upon, because it will take all your courage and good will to make this work. If you can't put that much of yourself into it, it would be best to forget it. As a marriage or partnership, there could be constant friction, since there would be little warmth or passion to ease the tension.

7 A complete meeting of the minds makes this an ideal relationship for two people of your nature. There should be no cause for misunderstanding or friction, and all will be smooth. All that is necessary is respect and honesty. You will both enjoy discussing subjects of a philosophical nature or those dealing with the occult. Literary pursuits are well favored. Professional writing can pay off well, and you might try coauthoring a book.

8 There should be no reason that you two cannot attain the highest of your material ambitions. The other person is the one with the executive mind and you should encourage him or her to do whatever is necessary to pursue your mutual goals. You are very logical and think things out wisely, while the other can take charge and get things done.

9 This is a peaceful and comfortable combination, and you should find much happiness together. All the necessary elements are here; sympathy, tolerance, understanding, and respect. You both enjoy probing into things to see what makes them tick, and therefore have great mental compatibility. You enjoy unusual subjects and are of one mind philosophically. There are strong psychic vibrations between you.

Destiny Number 8

Compatibility with Destiny Number:

1 What a dichotomous situation this can be! Either you will get along famously or hate each other with passion! You will both want your own way, and have the intelligence and experience to warrant it, so it will be difficult to know who will have to give in. If you can put personal ego aside, you could successfully join forces and achieve great things.

2 You are the bright spot in this relationship and cannot expect much excitement from the other person. However, you will have his or her full trust and cooperation, which is important if you realize this. You can go far with your experience and the assistance of your partner if you both recognize the other's qualities, and you don't try to suppress their practicality.

3 Since both parties in this relationship are intent upon attaining the same goals, you should find it an easy and comfortable one. What one person may lack, the other can supply, all of which makes for a strong and far-reaching partnership, whether in a business or personal sense. You are both vivacious, charming, and well liked by all, so you will be surrounded by adoring and appreciative friends.

4 There is an uncanny and unspoken understanding between you two that allows you to know without spoken words what the other is thinking or feeling. You anticipate each other's needs and are quick to respond. Your inventiveness and leadership contribute to this duo by balancing the strength and hard work of the other person. Great combination!

5 The 5-Person can get on your nerves and cause friction if you do not control your impulses. This person is more flighty and mercurial than you can handle, and your tendency will be to try to settle them down, which will not be appreciated. If you wish to pursue this relationship, you will have to overlook their flights of fancy and prattling.

6 You have great potential in the material sense, and the two of you can go to great heights if you give in a little and try to understand their motivation. They are quiet and given to concern for humanity, whereas you have great strength and get-up-and-go. Heed the desires and teachings of the other and you will learn much from them.

7 You can have a very good, well-balanced relationship if you recognize each other's potential. Where you are vibrant and quick acting when an idea occurs to you, the other person is slow to respond, intellectual, and contemplative. However, you need each other's strength, and it can be worked out favorably if you use diplomacy tendered with respect.

8 Here again, this relationship can go either way. There are explosive forces beneath the surface that can either tear it asunder or send it skyrocketing to the heights of success. You can be extremely successful and happy if you learn to accept compromise as your common ground. You are both brilliant and possess great executive ability. Give and take is the best rule for this pair, especially when it's done equally, and great progress results.

9 A good combination of intelligence, inventiveness, and executive ability mark this fortuitous combination and can bring great rewards. You have interests in many areas that can excite the other and you should try to involve them without inflicting your will on them. The other person has the strength and concentration to keep your relationship on a smooth and successful level, so you can happily sail into the sunset together.

Destiny Number 9

Compatibility with Destiny Number:

1 A very bright prospect for this combination. You are both creative, inventive, and original. There is no chance of boredom here, for you constantly search for new venues to explore and generally turn your prospects into success. The other person would be best at the helm and you will do very nicely alongside in most cases, lending creativity, encouragement, and excitement for a productive union.

2 You have the vivaciousness, curiosity, and keen sense of what is right for the two of you to make a go of this combination. The other person will aid and assist you in any way necessary, as 2 is the symbol of cooperation. You should have very pleasant sailing with few, if any, waves. You are both easy to get along with and enjoy each other's company in every aspect, so show your appreciation.

3 You must be careful and tread softly here because the other person may appear too gay and sociable at times when you might prefer concentration on some project if it is a business relationship, or a quiet evening of reading or television if a personal one, while your partner may prefer to be out and

about. Compromise is the key here and if you do so regularly, all should go smoothly, so don't worry.

4 A well-balanced duo; you have the fire of brilliant ideas and inventiveness to work out the details, while your mate has the practical knowledge and capability of implementing your plans. The total of 4 provides the stabilizing influence you may need at times; for when you are delirious with joy, they are more reserved, and vice versa; a perfect balance to keep you both on an even plane and content.

5 This can be a space-age combination because together you will soar to the heights of exciting adventure. Things will happen quickly, for neither of you has the desire or patience to linger over plans once you have set your sights. Both must try to see things rationally in order to make the most of your adventures and the resultant opportunities. Success will definitely be yours, as well as great adventures.

6 Two sensible, intelligent, and logical people make this a very comfortable combination, which should bring you the kind of peace and serenity you both want and need. You have no use for the games people play and can level with each other on anything. A wonderful foundation for any relationship. You will come to each other's aid whenever necessary, without request, and be happy to do so.

7 Both of you will find great pleasure and enrichment in this combination, for you will delight in being mutually helpful, encouraging each other and spurring each other on to new avenues of exploration. You have the same interests at heart and want the very same things out of life. You can help each other to attain these goals, and you will both be richer in every way by being together. It is also a very mystical combination and you could have interesting metaphysical experiences.

8 Your great thirst for knowledge and experiences keeps this relationship always exciting and interesting. The other person has the practical and executive sense that can turn your pursuits into profit. Let them take your ideas and help you mold them properly into a salable product or plan. In marriage you are the bright light and the other is the anchor, and you appreciate these traits in each other.

9 Wow—this is truly a power-plus combination! There can be no more fortuitous coupling for you than this one. You have been starred by fate to be extremely well matched in every way. You want all the same things and go about it in the same way. You both have strong powers of a psychic nature and an uncanny insight into all things occult, in a positive sense. Philosophy is also a subject of mutual interest and understanding, and you will share the great pleasure of exploring the mysteries of the universe together.

13

Personal Harmony by Name Expression

Have you ever met someone with whom you felt an immediate bond within moments of that meeting? Or do you have a friend whom you love dearly but could never go into business with? All of these experiences are quite natural in all our lives, and the reason is that the combined number total of the names involved gives strong vibrations of one sort or another that determines your relationship.

By using the Personal Harmony Vibration, you can tell at a glance just what is the best possible relationship you can expect. It may be that you are contemplating a business venture with someone whom, according to this chart, you would be better off confining to a social niche in your life.

To determine the type of relationship between two people, we add together their Name Expression numbers. To get the number of the Name Expression, print the names in full, exactly as they are known. If a nickname or title is always used, that is the way it should be computed. Ascribe to each letter the number found below it in the chart in chapter nine. For example: if we wish to compute the compatibility of Bill Clinton (remember, use the name by which the person is actually known, not necessarily their birth name) and Hillary Clinton:

```
B I L L   C L I N T O N
2 9 3 3   3 3 9 5 2 6 5 = 50

H I L L A R Y   C L I N T O N
8 9 3 3 1 9 7   3 3 9 5 2 6 5  = 73
```

Reduce these totals to a single digit: 50 becomes 5 because we drop the zero, so the vibration for Bill Clinton is 5. For Hillary Clinton add 7+3 for a total of 10; reduce to a single digit by dropping the zero and you have 1 for her vibration, with a combined value of 6. Look up 6 in the following charts to see their interaction with each other and what qualities each contributes.

To give just a very cursory overview of this combination, we see that President Clinton's 5-Vibration reflects the two main characteristics of the 5; always changing one's mind, and the gift of speech makes Clinton an excellent communicator. All 5s have a way with words, and as they say, "they can talk the socks off of you." These two characteristics are very much the image we have of President Clinton.

The 1-Vibration for Mrs. Clinton indicates the take-charge quality in her nature. She is widely seen as the one to dictate strategy when things got rough. However the combination of their two numbers becomes a 6-Vibration which stands for peace, family, and unity, and we know that their family unit comes first with them no matter what the problem. They are definitely a team, and as President Clinton said during his first campaign, "Elect one and you get two for your money." Since then they have shown this team spirit and unity, especially in the face of scandal, where tolerance on Mrs. Clinton's part was evident. She may not have liked the situation but to the public she showed total loyalty and cooperation in keeping up their image. Mrs. Clinton is an excellent mother and is concerned about all children, as is evidenced in her book, *It Takes a Village*. She has fought for insurance for everyone, for education, and all family issues.

Again, remember that this is just one form of determining compatibility. The Vowel and Consonant Vibrations plus the Destiny Number will color the picture a great deal.

Number 1 Vibration

Since 1 is the number of intellect and leadership, you have here a strong combination for power between you. You would do well in intellectual pursuits, both contributing equally to the forming of interests. Business would be strongly favored with two good heads at the helm. Collaboration in an intellectual sense should spawn many worthwhile and profitable concepts. Your creativity should be of value to various organizations as well as business. Charitable groups would benefit greatly with you two in command. Study and invention is also well favored. New ideas and methods devised by the two of you should be executed personally as you are both capable of performing these duties well together.

Number 2 Vibration

This is the perfect number for cooperation. Anything that relies heavily on this wonderful trait will be blessed. Marriage, of course, is perhaps the one relationship that requires more cooperation than any other, so here there should be no difficulty. In business you are best suited to something that does not require either of you to be the leader. You work extremely well together and can carry out the orders of your employer to the letter. This is an excellent indication for the diplomatic service or public relations. As coworkers on projects or in charitable groups you are indeed a great asset, seeking only to help rather than looking for glory. Together, you can build a lovely, charming home, or run the affairs of one without conflict. There is an equal amount of give and take here, which eliminates most problems.

Number 3 Vibration

With the strong power of self-expression inherent in the 3, there should always be fun and laughter wherever you are. Any of the performing arts would be ideal for the two of you. Entertaining will be your pleasure, and you will be known for your gay parties and company. A well-rounded, socially desirable couple, always in demand, you should never have difficulty in making friends. They will flock to you and bask in your charm. Anything to do with large groups of people will suit you; politics, public relations, financial endeavors, entertainment, charitable organizations, or the arts. You speak well—in fact, eloquently—and can therefore speak on behalf of anyone successfully. You would be successful in sales, training, or lectures. This is also a very sexually oriented duo, and the relationship can be quite passionate.

Number 4 Vibration

Hard work and tenacity symbolize a union such as this. You will both keep your noses to the grindstone; therefore, you would be an asset to any business. There will be no shilly-shallying here, and you will see that things get done on schedule and in proper order. There will be nothing left undone, or done in a slipshod manner. Building projects, research, finances, farming and business are most compatible to this combination. You can find success in anything you work at together with all your effort and concentration. This is best for a business relationship or as coworkers on some project. It is not necessarily a romantic combination, but, should there be one it will be less sentimental than perhaps others could be.

Number 5 Vibration

This can be a very active and adventuresome combination. You will be very much in the swim of things, always on the go, making new friends, having new experiences. Your relationship will be based on a foundation of change; change of business, location, home, relationships, ideas, or just about anything, because 5 always denotes change in some form or other. However, since this vibration applies to both of you, it can mean an exciting and adventuresome life. There will be no monotony or frugality to mar this relationship. With or without a cent in the bank, you will always find pleasure and excitement somewhere, without having to save laboriously for a two-week holiday in some dull, mundane place. Sales, writing, or anything to do with words and your projection of them will be successful.

Number 6 Vibration

Much love and happiness is destined for a couple with this Personal Harmony Number. Your home will be a happy one, your marriage a successful one, and your children happy and content in the atmosphere of charm and comfort that you create for them. The two of you will work well together in charitable organizations as 6 is the number of humanity and unselfishness. Educational pursuits, too, are destined here. Any course of study or teaching assignment would be a happy choice, and you will get on well together in this way. There is nothing that you wouldn't do for your fellow human, and you should be well blessed with the gratitude and respect of those you help. Financially, you see eye to eye, and there should be no problem on this score, for 6 is the number of peaceful resolution.

Number 7 Vibration

A most contemplative union, you will be happy with the silences that others cannot tolerate. You are both interested in pursuing the arts and the study of mystic subjects, such as astrology, numerology, hypnosis, and the like. It would be a relationship of intelligence, spirituality, and even perhaps moodiness. Speed would not be favorable here, since 7 is generally the number of deliberation and hesitation. This is not caused out of doubt but of serious thought before the deed. Beauty in some form would be necessary, if only in the surrounding view that you get in your home location. Physical activity is indicated in sports or games of some sort, but each move should be thoroughly thought out before it is made. You would serve well together in the field of medicine or some area where you could tend the sick.

Number 8 Vibration

What a blessed combination this is because 8 is always the number of fame, power, and fortune, so this duo would do well together in any financial matter, as they both have the same ideas about making money. There are some who will take every advantage in order to make a profit, but an 8 combination is too honest and respectable to do so. Your money-making projects will be worthy ones in which you handle yourselves honorably and cautiously, without intent to deprive anyone of their rights. Fairness and trust are very important to this combination, and 8s seek to sow charity wherever possible, giving of themselves and their finances. This trait of supreme justice augurs well for law careers or partners. Insurance and charitable organizations are also good avenues for the 8 combination.

Number 9 Vibration

This is a very exciting duo! A vast variety of experiences awaits this combination, and those who are open to new ideas and methods will be happy in such a situation. They will always have an urge to explore new countries or subjects and absorb everything they learn as a consequence, like sponges. The sign of the metaphysician is strong here, which indicates study of the mind or occult. Psychology or psychotherapy would be good fields for these two to be associated in, because they have the level of comprehension and interest in other people's problems that could make them very helpful. They are also broad-minded and curious enough to delve into unknown areas and try to find hidden answers in the interest of humanity. Scientific works, research, investigation, languages, charitable projects, or intellectual and adventurous pursuits are all areas in which these two would be compatible. Distances are favored, and they will most likely be extremely interested in foreign lands, peoples, and traveling.

14

Compatible Occupations

Since numerology can accurately pinpoint characteristics, personality traits, inherent powers, talent, and desires, it stands to reason that it is the ideal method by which to determine what careers or avocations you are best suited for and where success is most imminent. Why waste years of your life pursuing occupations for which you are clearly unsuited? Unfortunately, many of us go into our parents' established businesses or follow professions chosen by them, and do not wish to make them unhappy by insisting on following our own inclinations. This can be disastrous in more ways than one.

Often, too, there are those who really do not know what they want to do. Universities are loaded with students who still haven't made that all-important decision. Therefore, all those years and the money put into their education cannot be as effective or rewarding as choosing a definite vocation and keying their courses toward that end.

To find your Compatible Occupation use your Destiny Number: add together the day, month, and year of your birth and reduce the total to a single digit. Example: for the birth date of November 17, 1941, add 1+1 (November) +1 +7 (the date) +1+9+4+1 (the year) for a total of 25. Then reduce to a single digit: 2+5=7, which is the Destiny Number.

To find your Compatible Occupation, check the following sections. In this case you would check the 7. You will notice that many occupations reappear under several numbers, which is normal because the talents found in individual numbers are necessary in many occupations. A playwright, for instance, must be creative (number 3), he must also be capable of intense concentration (number 4), and have the gift of words (number 5), so don't be confused if your profession appears in several categories. It merely means that whatever your strong points are, you can make them work for you in various ways in your career, so you have quite a choice.

Compatible Occupation Number 1

A 1-Vibration lends itself well to executive positions, creative fields, and self-assured situations; so, obviously, this is where you would function most comfortably, happily, and successfully. Use your intuitive insight as a business executive, writer, ambassador, architect, designer, sales manager, neurologist, radio or TV station manager, film or radio director, advertising director, department head, attorney, surgeon, editor, psychiatrist, film producer, artist, actor, broker or moneylender, flyer, inventor, publicist or promoter, dean, explorer, army officer, personnel director, diagnostician, director of talent office or employment bureau, analyst, critic, newscaster, or politician. You need a field that allows you to experiment and to use your ability to the fullest. You must take the reins and be in a position of authority. Elaborate on every thought or idea.

Compatible Occupation Number 2

Any position that calls for utmost cooperation, understanding, diplomacy, and devotion to management would be the ideal setting for you. You function best when working in conjunction with others, rather than in a position of leadership; clerk, attorney, theatrical performer or producer, musician, writer, publisher, group organizer, second-in-command, tour director, real estate agent, desk clerk, receptionist secretary, bank clerk, correspondent, flight attendant, curator, exporter, cook, caterer, office assistant, girl Friday, policeman, engineer, any phase of the hotel or food business, manager of a chain operation, stenographer, collector, biographer, sculptor, politician, chorale member, or other musical occupation. Any way in which you can contribute cooperation and sincere interest will add to your vocational happiness.

Compatible Occupation Number 3

As this is the number of self-expression, you will obviously function most effectively where this expression can be of value. Positions in which you deal with the public at great length would be the most advantageous; judge, salesperson, publicity director, attorney, actor, writer, social correspondent, theatrical director or producer, playwright, photographer, model, politician, schoolteacher, cosmetician, hairdresser, designer, architect, landscape artist, interior decorator, nurse, physician, artist, clergyman, group leader, promoter, advertising director, children's group leader or Sunday school teacher, maitre d' or hostess, restaurant manager, anything to do with food or fashion, or an entertainer.

With the combination of expressiveness and creative talent given to a 3-Personality, you will always find contentment in fields of the arts and must never be relegated to less creative or exciting fields. Dealing with the public is paramount.

Compatible Occupation Number 4

You are the master of detail and hard, concentrated effort, so positions requiring such attributes will pay off handsomely for one of your caliber, which is rare. Leave the self-expression to others more flamboyant than you. You will do well as a builder, architect, mason, electrician, plumber, diagnostician, librarian, secretary, engineer, teacher, dean, inventor, farmer, horticulturist, draftsman, supervisor, banker, broker, army officer, critic, statistician, furniture designer or manufacturer, cashier or credit manager, surgeon, physician, buyer, store manager, playwright, economist, or economics teacher. Though some labors may seem mundane, your professionalism and attention to detail are a unique and revered quality and you must be proud of it.

Compatible Occupation Number 5

You will never be happy in a static position that keeps you forever tied down to one place or activity, for change is the spice of life for you. You will always have the urge to keep moving; as a travel agent, tour director, traveling salesperson, inspector, artist, writer, drama critic, theatrical director or producer, politician, sportsman, psychologist, analyst, photographer, theatrical agent, columnist, society reporter, publisher, sales promotion, publicity, linguist, reporter, editor, beauty expert, plastic surgeon, flyer, explorer, archaeologist, philosopher, politician, attorney, lecturer, literary agent, flight attendant, hostess, musician, dancer, playwright, or physical culturist. Develop an interest in or expertise in some active sport and certainly in travel if you are not so employed. With your keen sense of perception, you should meet and become involved with all manner of different people and groups to expand your interests.

Compatible Occupation
Number 6

As a very dependable and responsible person, you can always be relied upon to give of yourself and to transmit great sympathy and tolerance toward others. So a position requiring such assets would give you great satisfaction; teacher, psychologist, psychiatric, clergyman, nurse, physician, lecturer, hostess, flight attendant, actor, entertainment director, writer, editor, publisher, headmistress, dean, guidance counselor, camp counselor, Sunday-school teacher, personnel director, dancer, singer, wardrobe mistress, costume designer, landscape artist, cosmetologist, governess, interior decorator, fashion expert, hair stylist, group organizer, charity group director, theatrical designer, or physicist. Bring your sense of design and creativity into your home and build your hobbies around them; they could become a profitable sideline and a tension easer.

Compatible Occupation
Number 7

With your great powers of concentration, analysis, and perception, you will do well in any position requiring your complete attention and wisdom; researcher, personnel director, analyst, psychiatrist, psychologist, engineer, inventor, patent attorney, investment broker, market analyst, psychic investigator, historian, surgeon, scientist, archaeologist, physicist, explorer, judge, attorney, organizer, sportsman, mediator, counselor, navigator, astrologer, numerologist, character analyst, coin expert, designer, geologist, photographer, musician, doctor, clergyman, nun, religious expert, civic leader, surgeon, critic, editor, writer, model, or dean. You could easily become an authority on a wide variety of things, primarily on antique furniture, jewelry, coins, history, etiquette, or interior design. Research is your forte.

Compatible Occupation Number 8 *Tina*

Positions of responsibility, tact, and understanding will be ideal for you, and you should make the most of your abilities as material possessions can be yours if you work for them. You will do well as a charity worker, politician, inventor, executive, editor, writer, publisher, theatrical director or producer, banker, broker, military officer or expert, detective, crime investigator, manufacturer, critic, business analyst, dean, headmistress, librarian, sportsman, chemist, judge, attorney, sports counselor or coach, musical director, buyer, office manager, manager of restaurant, civil servant official, club organizer, collector, mechanic, or anything to do with philanthropical organizations. Combine your business acumen with charitable efforts, and it will be of mutual benefit to everyone. But allow yourself time for physical expression in some active manner, like sports competition, to balance your physical and mental exertion more evenly. Get out in the world, lend a strong helping hand to the less fortunate and make your mark.

Compatible Occupation
Number 9

A run-of-the-mill position will never suit you because you must be constantly in pursuit of new and exciting subjects. To pin you down in one static position would be too stifling. Your interest carries you into all fields and you do all things well; entertainer, philosopher, psychiatrist, analyst, writer, editor, publisher, artist, musician, psychic investigator, painter, publicist, public-relations expert, executive, inventor, idea person, research scientist, detective, surgeon, explorer, archaeologist, politician, historian, lecturer, radio or TV performer, theatrical director or producer, doctor, fashion expert, cosmetician, occult expert or medium, advertising director, sales director, travel expert, hair stylist, designer, decorator, or anything dealing with celebrities or important people. There are few limits, for someone such as you, so the world is your oyster. Delve into everything that triggers an interest and pass on your knowledge in some way to others. You will be a successful and happy individual.

15

Casting a Numeroscope

Now that you have all the basics in hand, it's time to learn how to put them all together and paint a total picture with all its shadings and details. You will see how the numbers interact with one another, strengthening some, negating others. A Total Personality Vibration may mean one thing when taken on its own, but something totally different when judged in conjunction with the Destiny Number or the power of either the vowel or consonant vibration. Let's use a fictitious couple to illustrate all the aspects we have learned within the covers of this book.

Elaine Kelly — Birth date: August 16, 1929
Robert Bradley — Birth date: April 3, 1929

Destiny Compatibility

Elaine: 8+1+6+1+9+2+9=36=9
Robert: 4+3+1+9+2+9=28=1

By combining the Destiny Numbers, 9 and 1, we have a total of 10, which reduces to 1. By this we can tell that Robert will definitely take the lead in this relationship because of his 1-Vibrancy, which gives him the power of leadership. He has ambition and intelligence, which promises a very successful career. It means too, that be will take control of the relationship as well, making all the decisions for the two of them. But Elaine will go along with him on just about anything since the vibrancy of her 9-Destiny makes her extremely agreeable. Her natural curiosity and adventuresome spirit allows her to delve into anything he should choose, because she enjoys the learning process of any project. She will be a great helpmate, urging him on, offering her own knowledge and suggestions, sharing his joy, feeding his ego, and lending her assistance eagerly. With her, it's doubtful that he would run into any resistance, and she, on the other hand, would be delighted with his strength, as 9s need mates with power and strength. There will be a good deal of exploration, creativity, and cooperation between these two, and they could quite easily reach the heights of success together.

Name Expression For Elaine

To determine personality compatibility with another person we have to take each factor into consideration; total vibrations for both parties, starting with our own. Using the same couple again we can now look at the whole picture.

```
 5   1 9   5      5        = 7 (HD)
 E L A I N E   K E L L Y
 3       2       5   3 3 7 =_5_(OE)
                          12 (TP)
```

Reduce 12 (1+2) to 3

We see by the Vowel Vibrancy 7, which tells us of her Heart's Desire (HD), that Elaine wishes she could be more introspective, methodical, spiritual, and thoughtful. She has a need of more carefully thought-out decisions, but this remains buried in her heart because the Consonant Vibrancy (OE, for Outward Expression) of number 5 makes her far too active, changeable, impulsive and vivacious to retreat within herself or to give more time to careful thinking. The 5 represents a love of the dramatic and need for acknowledgment, especially in artistic pursuits. She is very talented and constantly seeking applause.

Her Total Personality Vibration (TP), number 3, adds even more strength to her 5-Vibration, since it, too, revolves around the arts and self-expression. She would be extremely successful if she should seek a career in literature, drama, music, or any of the professions that require dealings with other people. Public relations, advertising or sales would be ideal if the arts are out of her reach.

The combination of the 5 and 3, both physical and sexual numbers, means that any relationship Elaine enters into will be an extremely passionate one, perhaps even indulging in the erotic if her mate agrees. Her sexuality is very important to her.

Now, add the above vibrations to her Destiny Number of 9, and you have a terrific combination of all that stands out in a crowd. She has an interest in absolutely everything, the curiosity and adventuresome spirit to explore all subjects and the self-expression to promote her interests. She wouldn't hesitate to pop off to the ends of the earth in pursuit of a new experience if the opportunity beckoned. She sees everything as a challenge and meets it head-on.

Name Expression For Robert

```
  6   5             1     5   = 17 (HD)
R O B E R T     B R A D L E Y
  9   2   9 2   2 9   4 3   7 = 47 (OE)

17 = 1+7 =           8 (HD)
47 = 4+7 = 11  =  2 (OE)
                10   =   1 (TP)
```

The 8 of Robert's Vowel Vibration shows that he has a strong desire for fame, power, and fortune. He wants to live a good life, with a beautiful home, luxury cars, and all the other trappings of success. The 2 of his consonants indicates that he has a good, easy way with people in that he is patient, tolerant, and cooperative, which helps tremendously in attaining his goals. At least we know that he will probably be blessed with loyalty from his employees since he knows how to treat them. This is a good sign because he needs a bit of a reining to hold back his natural tendency toward running roughshod over people, which is indicated by the 1 of his Destiny Number coupled with the 1 of his Total Personality Vibration. That's a pretty hard-nosed combination to stand up to, but the 2 does mitigate it somewhat. There is no doubt here that Robert will live up to his dreams of success because the double 1 of an 11 and the soul urge for fame, power, and fortune make it a certainty. This is a man who knows exactly what he wants and won't settle for a smidgen less.

Luckily for the two of them, Elaine's spirit and wide-open attitude blend beautifully with the rather restrictive nature of Robert's, which is just what he needs; interest, assistance, acceptance, and creative input. They each require and respect the attributes of the other.

Missing Links

Elaine lacks a 4, 6, and 9 in her name, which means that she does not have the perseverance she needs to help see her through all her many interests. She is apt to take up a project for a while and then drop it before completion because she loses interest. Robert's strong character and dedication to his purpose will help build that quality in her in time. Since she respects his strength, she will try to equal it. It is the nature of a 5 and 3. She also has no 6, signifying no true family interest. She would probably prefer to remain free of the restrictions of children. It also indicates that she finds it difficult to keep a lid on her temper and doesn't always see the other person's side of an argument. The role of peacemaker is not for her.

The lack of the number 8 proves that Elaine is not overly interested in the fame, power, and fortune as Robert is, therefore offering him no competition. There won't be a battle for supremacy here. She will be quite content to let him acquire these goals, while she concentrates on accolades. Her ego is more important to her, and she would be happy to receive acknowledgment for her artistic talents, rather than strictly financial rewards. At the same time, she will delight in Robert's expertise in acquiring all the assets of a beautiful life and will happily share them with him, embellishing them in her own special way, artistically and socially—just what Robert himself lacks and needs. With no missing links in his name, Robert proves to be a pretty well-rounded individual.

First Vowel Vibrancy

The "E" being the first vowel of Elaine's name indicates that she is perfectly in tune with the vibrations of her outward personality, which is also a 5, therefore having no inner personality conflicts. She knows exactly who she is and is quite content with that knowledge. She keeps nothing to herself and doesn't try to play games. Robert, on the other hand, develops a stronger sense of understanding and sympathy through the 6 power of his first vowel, the O. This allows him to be the perfect friend or mate and a most loving one at that. This is the perfect buffer for his personality, since the double 1 of the 11 could otherwise cause him to be extremely dictatorial and unfeeling. The O appearing where it does in his name lends him more strength than if it appeared elsewhere, which is ideal for him. This allows him to give Elaine the understanding she needs for her scattered thoughts and projects.

This gives you an idea of how to balance the powers of all the patterns we have discussed. With this kind of knowledge, you should be able to plot the personality and destiny of anyone with a reasonable amount of accuracy. Needless to say, you will leave mouths agape when you show off your skill.

Name Changes

As we have seen in previous chapters, we can tell almost everything just from a name—each letter vibrating to certain numbers and spotlighting specific traits. The logical question then is what happens when a woman marries and changes her name. Let's use the couple from our numeroscope to see how Elaine Kelly would make this transition if she became Elaine Bradley. First, we must recalculate the vibrations. Originally they were;

Elaine's:	Robert's:
7 Hearts Desire	8 Heart's Desire
5 Outward Expression	2 Outward Expression
3 Total Personality	3 Total Personality

Now we redo Elaine's name as Elaine Bradley:

$5+1+9+1+5=26=2+6=8$

So now Elaine's Total Personality Vibration is a 5 instead of 3. It is easy to see that after marriage, Bob's strong 1-Vibrancy, which requires total control, has managed to change Elaine's personality to coincide, and I'm sure the marriage would be a happy one as a result. The 5 of her new Total Personality indicates the patience, tolerance, and cooperation that Bob needs, and which makes the change so easy for her.

Bob's Heart's Desire, number 9, has now become Elaine's, which indicates that she wishes to help him attain all his goals. This means she has molded her overall personality to absorb and blend with his. Yet the 3 of the Total Personality of her maiden name now recedes to the position of her Outward Expression, and doubles by becoming a 6, indicating that she has subdued her natural flamboyance to complement Robert's more conservative nature. A perfect blend for a perfect couple.

You can achieve the same thing if certain vibrations of your name are restricting your personality, success, or relationships. By adding or subtracting certain letters, you can change your vibrations, and it's a certainty your life will change as a result. This is obvious in our example with Elaine and Robert.

Various number combinations can cause too many problems. For instance; an 11 Total Personality (before reducing it to 2) combined with an 11 Destiny Number can make you extremely difficult to get along with, overly critical, and not well liked. A 5-Vowel and a 5-Consonant power could indicate too much fickleness and no concentration of efforts, which makes life very unstable and difficult to cope with. A 1-Vowel and 1-Consonant with perhaps a 1-Destiny becomes a far too dictatorial and domineering woman who therefore finds romance to be quite elusive. On the opposite side of the coin, a man with all 2s lacks the strength, drive, and determination to get ahead in business. If one's dream is of fame, power, and fortune, the 8-Vibrancy is necessary, and can be achieved by rearranging the name until the Total Personality comes out to the all-important 8.

These changes can be made in many ways: usually dropping an initial, changing the spelling of the first name or using a diminutive of the name can effect it. For example, I changed my first name from Geri to Gerie. John can become Jon, Lucy can be changed to Lucie; Cathy to Kathy, Kathie, or Kath; Joan can switch to Jonne or Joanne. Just play with it and eventually you'll come up with something that suits you and at the same time gives you the vibration you wish.

One thing I can promise you, whether you accept numerology as the true science that it is, or just as a fun thing to do, you can't avoid being impressed with its accuracy. You will find yourself delving ever deeper into its exciting intricacies to discover very special "magic powers."

☾ ORDER LLEWELLYN BOOKS TODAY!

Llewellyn publishes hundreds of books on your favorite subjects! To get these exciting books, including the ones on the following pages, check your local bookstore or order them directly from Llewellyn.

Order Online:
Visit our website at www.llewellyn.com, select your books, and order them on our secure server.

Order by Phone:
- Call toll-free within the U.S. at 1-877-NEW-WRLD (1-877-639-9753). Call toll-free within Canada at 1-866-NEW-WRLD (1-866-639-9753)
- We accept VISA, MasterCard, and American Express

Order by Mail:
Send the full price of your order (MN residents add 7% sales tax) in U.S. funds, plus postage & handling to:

Llewellyn Worldwide
P.O. Box 64383, Dept. 1-56718-057-4
St. Paul, MN 55164-0383, U.S.A.

Postage & Handling:
Standard (U.S., Mexico, & Canada). If your order is:
Up to $25.00, add $3.50
$25.01 - $48.99, add $4.00
$49.00 and over, FREE STANDARD SHIPPING
(Continental U.S. orders ship UPS. AK, HI, PR, & P.O. Boxes ship USPS 1st class. Mex. & Can. ship PMB.)

International Orders:
Surface Mail: For orders of $20.00 or less, add $5 plus $1 per item ordered. For orders of $20.01 and over, add $6 plus $1 per item ordered.

Air Mail:
Books: Postage & Handling is equal to the total retail price of all books in the order.
Non-book items: Add $5 for each item.

Orders are processed within 2 business days. Please allow for normal shipping time. Postage and handling rates subject to change.

ASTROLOGY FOR BEGINNERS

An Easy Guide to Understanding & Interpreting Your Chart

William W. Hewitt

Anyone who is interested in astrology will enjoy *Astrology for Beginners*. This book makes astrology easy and exciting by presenting all of the basics in an orderly sequence while focusing on the natal chart. Llewellyn even includes a coupon for a free computerized natal chart so you can begin interpretations almost immediately without complicated mathematics.

Astrology for Beginners covers all of the basics. Learn exactly what astrology is and how it works. Explore signs, planets, houses and aspects. Learn how to interpret a birth chart. Discover the meaning of transits, predictive astrology and progressions. Determine your horoscope chart in minutes without using math.

Whether you want to practice astrology for a hobby or aspire to become a professional astrologer, *Astrology for Beginners* is the book you need to get started on the right track.

0–87542–307–8, 288 pp., 5¼ x 8   **$9.95**

AURA READING FOR BEGINNERS

Develop Your Psychic Awareness for Health & Success

Richard Webster

When you lose your temper, don't be surprised if a dirty red haze suddenly appears around you. If you do something magnanimous, your aura will expand. Now you can learn to see the energy that emanates off yourself and other people through the proven methods taught by Richard Webster in his psychic training classes.

Learn to feel the aura, see the colors in it, and interpret what those colors mean. Explore the chakra system, and how to restore balance to chakras that are over- or under-stimulated. Then you can begin to imprint your desires into your aura to attract what you want in your life.

These proven methods for seeing the aura will help you: interpret the meanings of colors in the aura; find a career that is best suited for you; relate better to the people you meet and deal with; enjoy excellent health; discover areas of your life that you need to work on; imprint what you want in your future into your aur; make aura portraits with pastels or colored pencils; discover the signs of impending ill health, drug abuse, and pain; change the state of your aura and stimulate specific chakras through music, crystals, color; see what the next few weeks or months are going to be like for you

1–56718–798–6, 208 pp., 5³⁄₁₆ x 8, illus.   **$9.95**

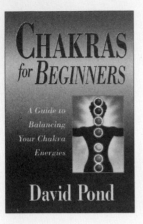

CHAKRAS FOR BEGINNERS
A Guide to Balancing Your Chakra Energies

David Pond

The chakras are spinning vortexes of energy located just in front of your spine and positioned from the tailbone to the crown of the head. They are a map of your inner world—your relationship to yourself and how you experience energy. They are also the batteries for the various levels of your life energy. The freedom with which energy can flow back and forth between you and the universe correlates directly to your total health and well-being.

Blocks or restrictions in this energy flow expresses itself as disease, discomfort, lack of energy, fear, or an emotional imbalance. By acquainting yourself with the chakra system, how they work and how they should operate optimally, you can perceive your own blocks and restrictions and develop guidelines for relieving entanglements.

The chakras stand out as the most useful model for you to identify how your energy is expressing itself. With *Chakras for Beginners* you will discover what is causing any imbalances, how to bring your energies back into alignment, and how to achieve higher levels of consciousness.

1–56718–537–1, 216 pp., 5³⁄₁₆ x 8 $9.95

DOWSING FOR BEGINNERS

The Art of Discovering: Water, Treasure, Gold, Oil, Artifacts

Richard Webster

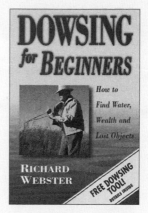

This book provides everything you need to know to become a successful dowser. Dowsing is the process of using a dowsing rod or pendulum to divine for anything you wish to locate: water, oil, gold, ancient ruins, lost objects or even missing people. Dowsing can also be used to determine if something is safe to eat or drink, or to diagnose and treat allergies and diseases.

Learn about the tools you'll use: angle and divining rods, pendulums, wands—even your own hands and body can be used as dowsing tools! Explore basic and advanced dowsing techniques, beginning with methods for dowsing the terrain for water. Find how to dowse anywhere in the world without leaving your living room, with the technique of map dowsing. Discover the secrets of dowsing to determine optimum planting locations; to monitor your pets' health and well-being; to detect harmful radiation in your environment; to diagnose disease; to determine psychic potential; to locate archeological remains; to gain insight into yourself, and more! *Dowsing for Beginners* is a complete "how-to-do-it" guide to learning an invaluable skill.

1–56718–802–8, 256 pp., 5¼ x 8, illus., photos $12.95

FENG SHUI FOR BEGINNERS

Successful Living by Design

Richard Webster

Not advancing fast enough in your career? Maybe your desk is located in a "negative position." Wish you had a more peaceful family life? Hang a mirror in your dining room and watch what happens. Is money flowing out of your life rather than into it? You may want to look to the construction of your staircase!

For thousands of years, the ancient art of feng shui has helped people harness universal forces and lead lives rich in good health, wealth and happiness. The basic techniques in *Feng Shui for Beginners* are very simple, and you can put them into place immediately in your home and work environments. Gain peace of mind, a quiet confidence, and turn adversity to your advantage with feng shui remedies.

1–56718–803–6, 240 pp., 5¼ x 8, photos, diagrams   **$12.95**

HYPNOSIS FOR BEGINNERS

Reach New Levels of Awareness & Achievement

William W. Hewitt

Hypnosis is one of the most valuable tools available for the enrichment of lives. It's a normal, safe, healthy phenomenon that brings you to the altered state of consciousness needed for directing your mind to specific goals. The power and scope of self hypnosis can blow your mind into new, heightened levels of awareness and achievement.

When you are finished with this step-by-step guide, you will be able to hypnotize yourself and others safely and easily. Whether your goal is to stop smoking, control migraine headaches or commune with your spirit guides, you will find hypnosis routines that you can use for any purpose, including special tips for hypnosis with children. In addition, you will be able to record your own audiotapes to regress yourself into past lives. Several case histories from the author's own clientele dramatically illustrate the power of this remarkably simple yet profound technique.

1–56718–359–X, 288 pp., 5³⁄₁₆ x 8   **$9.95**

MAGICK FOR BEGINNERS
The Power to Change Your World

J. H. Brennan

Many magicians wear a great cloak, "the aura of dark mystery," which J. H. Brennan endeavors to remove in *Magick for Beginners*. In doing so, he introduces many aspects of magic and the occult, and explains in detail several experiments which you can try for yourself, including producing a $100 bill by magic, and becoming invisible.

The book is divided into two parts: Low Magick and High Magick. In Low Magick you will explore the Ouija board, astral and etheric bodies, the chakras, the aura, Qabalah, wood nymphs and leprechauns, mantra chanting, water and ghost divining, and the Tree of Life. Low Magick is fun, and serves as an introduction to the more potent system of High Magick. Here you will learn how to correctly prepare your mind before conducting ritual magic, and how to conduct the rituals themselves.

1–56718–086–8, 336 pp., 5³⁄₁₆ x 8, illus. $9.95

REIKI FOR BEGINNERS
Mastering Natural Healing Techniques

David F. Vennels

Reiki is a simple, yet profound, system of hands-on healing developed in Japan during the 1800s. Millions of people worldwide have already benefited from its peaceful healing intelligence that transcends cultural and religious boundaries. It can have a profound effect on health and well-being by re-balancing, cleansing, and renewing your internal energy system.

Reiki for Beginners gives you the very basic and practical principles of using Reiki as a simple healing technique, as well as its more deeply spiritual aspects as a tool for personal growth and self-awareness. Unravel your inner mysteries, heal your wounds, and discover your potential for great happiness. Follow the history of Reiki, from founder Dr. Mikao Usui's search for a universal healing technique, to the current development of a global Reiki community. Also included are many new ideas, techniques, advice, philosophies, contemplations, and meditations that you can use to deepen and enhance your practice.

1–56718–767–6, 264 pp., 5³⁄₁₆ x 8, illus.   **$12.95**

SCRYING FOR BEGINNERS
Tapping into the Supersensory Powers of Your Subconscious

Donald Tyson

Scrying for Beginners is for anyone who longs to sit down before the mirror or crystal and lift the rolling grey clouds that obscure their depths. Scrying is a psychological technique to deliberately acquire information by extrasensory means through the unconscious mind. For the first time, all forms of scrying are treated in one easy-to-read, practical book. They include such familiar methods as crystal gazing, pendulums, black mirrors, Ouija boards, dowsing rods, aura reading, psychometry, automatic writing and automatic speaking. Also treated are ancient techniques not widely known today, such as Babylonian oil scrying, fire gazing, Egyptian lamp scrying, water scrying, wind scrying, ink scrying, shell-hearing, and oracular dreaming. Includes special offer for a free scrying sheet

1–56718–746–3, 320 pp., 5³⁄₁₆ x 8, illus. $12.95

TAROT FOR BEGINNERS

An Easy Guide to Understanding & Interpreting the Tarot

P. Scott Hollander

The Tarot is much more than a simple divining tool. While it can—and does—give you accurate and detailed answers to your questions when used for fortune-telling, it can also lead you down the road to self-discovery in a way that few other meditation tools can do. Tarot for Beginners will tell you how to use the cards for meditation and self-enlightenment as well as for divination.

If you're just beginning a study of the Tarot, this book gives you a basic, straightforward definition of the meaning of each card that can be easily applied to any system of interpretation, with any Tarot deck, using any card layout. The main difference between this book and other books on the Tarot is that it's written in plain English—you need no prior knowledge of the Tarot or other arcane subjects to understand its mysteries, because this no-nonsense guide will make the symbolism of the Tarot completely accessible to you. You will receive an overview of the cards of the Major and Minor Arcana in terms of their origin, purpose and interpretive uses as well as clear, in-depth descriptions and interpretations of each card.

1–56718–363–8, 352 pp., 5¼ x 8, illus.   **$12.95**

Astral Travel for Beginners
Transcend Time and Space with Out-of-Body Experiences
Richard Webster

Astral projection, or the out-of-body travel, is a completely natural experience. You have already astral traveled thousands of times in your sleep, you just don't remember it when you wake up. Now, you can learn how to leave your body at will, be fully conscious of the experience, and remember it when you return.

The exercises in this book are carefully graded to take you step-by-step through an actual out-of-body experience. Once you have accomplished this, it becomes easier and easier to leave your body. That's why the emphasis in this book is on your first astral travel.

The ability to astral travel can change your life. You will have the freedom to go anywhere and do anything. You can explore new worlds, go back and forth through time, make new friends, and even find a lover on the astral planes. Most importantly, you will find that you no longer fear death as you discover that you are indeed a spiritual being independent of your physical body.

1-56718-796-X, 256 pp., 5 ³⁄₁₆ x 8   **$9.95**

LOVE NUMBERS
How to Use Numerology to Make Love Count

Margaret Arnold

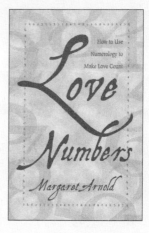

Why do some relationships work and others fail? Why do you immediately like some people while others leave you feeling cold? Why do you click with someone, even when it appears by worldly standards that you shouldn't?

The answer to these questions lies in the interrelationships of the energy patterns, called vibrations, that make up our bodies and personalities. One way to understand and analyze these patterns is through the science of numerology.

With a knowledge of numerical vibrations you can know ahead of time how your own and another person's personalities will interact. If you're a 4, for example, you want dependability, order, and structure—and you will want to avoid 5s, which crave change and lots of freedom. You'd be better off with an 8 because you can both be very hard workers. This book gives you all the simple formulas you need to determine the numerology for anyone.

1–56718–040–X, 304 pp., 5³⁄₁₆ x 8   **$9.95**

PALM READING FOR BEGINNERS

Find the Future in the Palm of Your Hand

Richard Webster

Announce in any gathering that you read palms and you will be flocked by people thrilled to show you their hands. When you are have finished *Palm Reading for Beginners*, you will be able to look at anyone's palm (including your own) and confidently and effectively tell them about their personality, love life, hidden talents, career options, prosperity, and health.

Palmistry is possibly the oldest of the occult sciences, with basics principles that have not changed in 2,600 years. This step-by-step guide clearly explains the basics, as well as advanced research conducted in the past few years on such subjects as dermatoglyphics.

1-56718-791-9, 5³⁄₁₆ x 8, 264 pp., illus., softcover $9.95

TO ORDER, CALL 1-800-THE MOON
Prices subject to change without notice.

REFLEXOLOGY FOR BEGINNERS

Healing through Foot Massage of Pressure Points

David Vennells

Reflexology is one of the most well known and well respected complementary therapies. It is even practiced in many hospitals, hospices, and healing centers. The principles of practical reflexology are quite simple. This book puts reflexology back into the hands of those who have a heartfelt wish to help themselves and others.

Reflexology can have a profound effect on our health and well-being by re-balancing, cleansing, and renewing our internal energy system. As you learn the techniques step-by-step, you will gradually increase your knowledge of anatomy and physiology, while developing a more accurate awareness of the foot reflexes and how to treat them.

- Written by a professional reflexologist

- Within a week or even a few days, you will be able to give your first full reflexology treatments

- This book also presents reflexology as a therapy for mental and emotional healing

0-7387-0098-3, 5 ³⁄₁₆ x 8, 288 pp., illus. $9.95

PSYCHIC DEVELOPMENT FOR BEGINNERS

An Easy Guide to Releasing & Developing Your Psychic Abilities

William Hewitt

Psychic Development for Beginners provides detailed instruction on developing your sixth sense, or psychic ability. Improve your sense of worth, your sense of responsibility and therefore your ability to make a difference in the world. Innovative exercises like "The Skyscraper" allow beginning students of psychic development to quickly realize personal and material gain through their own natural talent.

Benefits range from the practical to spiritual. Find a parking space anywhere, handle a difficult salesperson, choose a compatible partner, and even access different time periods! Practice psychic healing on pets or humans—and be pleasantly surprised by your results. Use psychic commands to prevent dozing while driving. Preview out-of-body travel, cosmic consciousness and other alternative realities. Instruction in *Psychic Development for Beginners* is supported by personal anecdotes, 44 psychic development exercises, and 28 related psychic case studies to help students gain a comprehensive understanding of the psychic realm.

1-56718-360-3, 5¼ x 8, 216 pp., softcover   **$9.95**